Fire Up Your Communication Skills

Get People to Listen, Understand, and Give You What You Want!

"Captain Bob"

Second Edition

CODE 3 PUBLISHING, PLEASANTON, CALIFORNIA

Fire Up Your Communication Skills
Get People to Listen, Understand,
and Give You What You Want!

by "Captain Bob"

Published by:
Code 3 Publishing
5565 Black Avenue
Pleasanton, CA 94566

Publisher's Cataloging-in-Publication
(Provided by Quality Books, Inc.)

Smith, Bob, (Robert Ernest), 1941
    Fire up your communication skills : get people to listen,
understand, and give you what you want! / Captain Bob. — 2nd ed.
    p. cm.
    Includes bibliographical references and index.
    Preassigned LCCN: 97-091681
    ISBN: 0-9657620-6-8

       1. Communication in marriage. 2. Interpersonal
communication. I. Title.

BF637.C45S65 1977   302.2
                                       QBI97-40566

DEDICATION

*This book is for the family who was still there
when I changed — Harriet, Rob and Stu.
It's also for those who have the courage to change.*

Contents

Contents 7

Who Is Captain Bob?

His real name is Bob Smith and he's a fireman. He's married and he has kids. He likes sports and he goes to church regularly and he owns a home with a nice lawn and he has friendly neighbors.

Bob Smith. Plain ol' Bob Smith.

Routine name. Routine guy. Routine life.

Bob has always been a lot like you and a lot like me. Solid-as-a-rock Bob. Good-old-dependable Bob. Steady-as-she-goes Bob. No-cares-in-the-world Bob. Right?

. . . well . . . not really.

Bob had a problem. He didn't know he had this problem, but it was there nonetheless. And it was a big problem. It was a problem that was as mysterious as cancer, as dangerous as crocodile wrestling, and as powerful and as deadly as the huge fires Bob was often called upon to battle against.

His problem was *ignorance regarding maintenance of communication and love relationships.*

Bob wasn't a wife beater, but neither was he a wife pleaser. Bob wasn't a callous-hearted man, but neither was he an open-hearted man. Bob wasn't a demanding man, but neither was he an attentive man.

Bob was just Bob. He worked steadily, brought home a paycheck, cut his grass, washed his car, went to Sunday school, took his wife to dinner on their anniversary and played ball with his sons. He was never cruel, but he was always ignorant.

Bob stayed ignorant of his wife's deepest needs as a person until one day he asked her if she was happy with their marriage. His wife Harriet said it was a "good" marriage. It could have been a lot better, however.

This amazed Bob. He thought that he had been doing everything "by the book." And, the truth was, he had. Unfortunately, Bob had read the wrong book.

When Bob tried to find the "right" book, he discovered that it hadn't been written yet. So, he learned his lessons by trial and error, experiment and correction, progress and setback. And once he had learned what it took to make his relationship with his wife better, he shared these insights with other people. And they, too, improved their relationships.

Did Bob earn a Ph.D. in psychology? Nope. Did Bob have many years of training as a counselor? Nope. Did Bob have a research staff that helped him do long-range group studies? Nope.

The only things Bob had were the right answers regarding how to strengthen loving relationships. But then again, that's all people wanted.

So now Bob has "written the book" on this subject. You can read it and start to live your life "by the book"—the *right* book this time.

Dr. Dennis E. Hensley
author of *Uncommon Sense* and
How to Stop Living for the Applause

Acknowledgment

To my editor, Dr. Dennis Hensley, who added much and presented my writing the way I speak. He became a friend in the process.

For the support and encouragement of lifelong friend Dan Poynter. He knew I could do this when I had doubts. He provided the road map that got me to the final destination.

Special thanks and appreciation to John Gottman, Ph.D., for sharing his years of research so others could benefit.

To my wonderful wife, Harriet, who labored beside me during this book birthing. Also, for her help in resurrecting four chapters you would otherwise not be reading because I had sent them in error to deletion obscurity.

To Bill Davenport, who was an early mentor.

For my assistant, Mary Richart, who kept me on track.

To the many who shared the stories of their journeys to capture peace and happiness.

I sincerely thank all these fine people. I know they are proud of their contribution to this work.

And lastly, I wish to acknowledge those authors whose names I was not able to identify with the quotes and sayings that I share in this book. They have offered me much hope and wisdom over the years, and I trust they will provide you with the same.

Copyediting by Gail Kearns
Book design by Christine Nolt of Cirrus Design
Cover by Gaelyn Larrick of Lightbourne Images

Warning-Disclaimer

This book is designed to provide information in regard to the subject matter covered. It is sold with the understanding that the publisher and author are not engaged in rendering legal, accounting, psychological, or other professional services. If legal or other expert assistance is required, the services of a competent professional should be sought.

It is not the purpose of this book to reprint all the information that is otherwise available to the author and/or publisher, but to complement, amplify and supplement other texts. You are urged to read all the available material, learn as much as possible about communication and relationships, and tailor the information to your individual needs.

The author is not licensed to practice psychology. This text is not intended to replace psychological counseling; it is simply a communication and relationship philosophy based on the author's, and countless others, experiences.

Every effort has been made to make this book as complete and as accurate as possible. However, there may be mistakes both typographical and in content. Therefore, this text should be used only as a general guide and not as the ultimate source on communication and relationship information. Furthermore, this book contains information on communication and relationships only up to the printing date.

The purpose of this book is to educate and entertain. The author and Code 3 Publishing shall have neither liability nor responsibility to any person or entity with respect to any loss or damage caused, or alleged to be caused, directly or indirectly by the information contained in this book.

If you do not wish to be bound by the above, you may return this book to the publisher for a full refund.

From the Author

For those of you who are not too sure that you really want to read all this communication and relationship stuff, try the condensed version of this book. There are eleven short-burst chapters marked by an asterisk in the table of contents and with the chapter displays themselves. These chapters will give you a quick idea as to whether or not you'll want to read further. We don't want anyone to be taken hostage, kicking and screaming all the way.

Note on confidentiality: All the material in this book has been carefully disguised to protect confidentiality. All names of subjects are fictitious. No person may be identified from material presented herein.

Chapter 1

✳ Learn the Nuggets of Life

I love the scene in a hit movie in which a private investigator is in the office of a woman police lieutenant. They are arguing. Finally, she says, "You know, I could make your life a living hell." His reply is, "No, thank you, I'm not interested in a serious relationship right now."

Actually, most people want to have good communication skills and be involved in good relationships. And those people who have a good balance of communication and relationship skills at home and in business are the most successful and have the happiest lives. There is a direct overlap between home and business.

We arrive in our relationships without the tools or owner manuals for these six major areas: communication, relationships, marriage, sex, children, and money. Nevertheless, we attempt to proceed through life as though we are experts in each category. No wonder we often fail. Sometimes, the toughest lesson to learn is really the one we thought we already had learned.

But change can occur rapidly where there are skills, tools, and the Nuggets of Life that you did not know were there. Some of them are already inside you. Then, suddenly there is new hope and optimism over the fact that your communication and relationships can improve. And they will! Because these Nuggets of Life produce their own energy. A Nugget of

Life is something that changes your life but not necessarily your circumstances, such as a change in attitude. Attitude is your rudder through life.

What is a firefighter doing here writing about communication and relationships? Believe me, it's not one of the hot topics at the fire house. Hey, we're in a macho profession. This is a tough and demanding job. We're heroes. One word got me here . . . Pain! In my twenty-second year of marriage with my wife Harriet, things were at the breaking point. I had plenty of skill for my dangerous job fighting fires, but few useful skills for communication and relationships. We get few tools from our parents and we pass even fewer on to our children. This is truly one of the "sins of the generations."

As I started out to overcome my weak areas, I found that I wasn't the only one needing help. I was among the multitudes who had the same problems in communication and relationships. As I gained new skills, I was asked to speak and share my insights with others. The sharing has continued for more than twelve years.

What we're talking about here is the ability to recognize and understand the differences between folks and to use simple tools to uncomplicate our lives. Just minor changes in you can make major differences in your relationships.

We are dramatically, dramatically, dramatically different in incalculable ways. Is there anyone who hasn't figured this one out yet? Knowing this, we need as many of the Nuggets of Life as possible to help us get to the areas of intimacy and happiness we all say we are looking for.

This also applies to single people who say, "Well, first I just want someone to stand still long enough to get a relationship started." These tools can help you to strengthen your position and enable you to *provide* more when it comes to establishing a relationship.

The Nuggets of Life that will be presented in this book are for anyone interested in establishing good communication skills and in strengthening and maintaining relationships. What's great is that these new talents can be accomplished without changing who you really are. You might need to adjust your course a little.

🔥   *Attitude is such a small thing that can make a big difference.*

Before moving on, I'd like to add these disclaimers:

- Don't take everything in this book too seriously.
- It's not the intent of this book to attack either men or women.
- I'm not trying to stereotype men or women. What I write will apply to about 80% of the population. If it doesn't apply to you, that's fine. Don't get mad.
- Yes, men and women play multiple roles. If you identify with something that was written about the opposite gender and it applies to you, that's okay, too.
- This book wasn't written to tell men and women how they are supposed to feel, think, or act. That would be impossible. Take what might work for you and leave the rest.
- The book is not a prescription for happiness. Only you can supply that.

I was able to improve my communication and relation-ships with my family and others by using the information con-tained in this book. Countless others have had the same success. It is my hope that you will walk away with at least a few of these Nuggets of Life and that they will provide an easier journey along the way to improved communication and better relationships.

🔥   *Happiness is not a destination. It's a form of travel.*

Chapter 2

✳ The Communication Class

My wife Harriet and I were taking a couple's communication class. On one particular Sunday there was a lot of tension in the air. I asked the instructor Ken if we could stop and individually write down a number from one to ten (ten being the best) where we thought our marriages or current relationships were. He agreed to let us do it. (What I since learned is that men will usually rate their relationship three to four points higher than women.) Then he asked if someone wanted to share. One fellow said, "I will. I think my marriage is between a nine and a ten." At that point his wife whipped around with daggers in her eyes and said, "What could you have been thinking? Why do you think we're here taking this class? I just put down a three." She proceeded to tell us that she thought they were headed for a divorce. This set the tone for the rest of the couples in the room. Few were close to their partner's number.

I thought, *something is going on here that I need to know about.* A few days later I took Harriet to a nice place for lunch. I asked her if she could tell me those things that made her feel special or loved. If she didn't know right then, a few days later would be fine. I didn't have to wait. As I was to find out with most women, the computer didn't go searching. In a nanosecond, Harriet started telling me what made her feel loved.

There were five things. I knew, perhaps, one of them; I

didn't have a clue as to the other four. In other words, if I was strapped into the electric chair to be executed and all I had to do to save my life was come up with the five things that made my wife feel loved, they would have thrown the switch long ago. I didn't know.

What I had discovered for myself was that my wife had a Love Bank that contained those special things that made her feel loved. You have one, too. We all do.

Actually, the Love Bank has always been there. Don't you remember the times when that special person in your life had a Love Bank that became overdrawn . . . and you didn't have overdraft protection? Oh, yeah, you remember.

I decided to take those five things my wife told me that made her feel loved and to start using them to open a Love Bank Account. It was just like going down to the bank and opening up a savings account.

I started making deposits in my wife's Love Bank Account by doing those things that made her feel special and loved. I quickly found out that it was an interest and dividend earning account. Guess who got the dividends from this account? Right: **me!** It turned out to be the largest interest I had ever received (in those things that made *me* feel loved), and I didn't even have to report it to the IRS. You can also open up a Love Bank Account.

I have noticed that we cruise through life for the most part not really knowing what makes those special people in our lives feel loved. Because men and women are wired so dramatically differently (you have noticed, haven't you?), we think we are sending the message out as to what makes us feel loved. But the message seems to get lost in the translation and comes out as gibberish. And when we don't know what really makes that person feel special and loved, **we are shooting at a mov-**

ing target. As such, we end up doing for others what makes *us* feel loved. It's not the same. Love Bank deposits send the message that you care. They provide new Nuggets of Life, tools and skills in your tool box for improving and repairing relations.

There are people who would say that this is phony, it's giving in, being weak, knuckling under and giving up control (as if they had it). I disagree. It's like Sears coming out with a new tool for your trade or a new program for your computer. When computers first went in at my job, it took over one hour to do my first report. Now I can do the same report in less than one minute. To master these new tools and skills, there is a learning period that takes time. But once you master the new skills and tools, it makes your job easier. Tools for a carpenter make his job easier. Communication and relationship tools will make your life easier. When you are in a healthy relationship with good skills and tools, it's doing easy time. When there are few tools or skills to deal with unresolved issues in an unhealthy relationship, it's like doing hard time in prison.

Example: After five years of marriage, Bill is not happy because their sex life is not what it was. Donna has emotionally shut down to Bill because she feels that there is no opportunity for growth and hope in their relationship. Bill won't take the time to listen or talk to Donna. Donna feels shut out and frustrated because she can't express her feelings and is not being accepted by Bill. Donna nags Bill, unconsciously thinking it will make Bill fulfill her needs. This is *hard time*. So, you see, you can do hard time or you can do easy time. The choice is yours. I ask people at my speaking engagements, "How many of you want to sign up for doing hard time?" Silence. No one raises his or her hand. Then I say, "How come so many of you are on death row?"

Unfortunately, you can't just go out and buy a new set of communication and relationship tools. Even if you could, you wouldn't know how to use them. It would be like giving you a complete set of electrician's tools and sending you out to make a repair. Without the skills, you wouldn't be able to do it. It's the same with communication and relationship tools. It takes time, work and commitment to obtain the skills for a relationship to work well.

At first, some women consider this Love Bank and tools-for-relationship concept as being too mechanical. I can assure you that if you will continue on this journey for a few more chapters, just around the next bend it will all start making sense.

Why would a person who wants to improve his or her communication skills and relationships keep using the same tools that produce the wrong results?

So, what have you done or what are you now doing that has worked? Isn't it time to trade in those old, outdated tools and skills for the new, state-of-the-art, cutting edge communication and relationship tools? The only thing you need in order to get started is a desire and willingness to learn. Without these, don't bother. You might say, "Well, that's just the way I am. I've always been this way. I can't change." "Can't" means "won't." "Can't" might find you living somewhere else.

      🔥   *Knock the 't' off the can't.*
          —George Reeves (1876–1925)

  🔥   *The world is moving so fast these days that the man who says it can't be done is generally interrupted by someone doing it.*
          —Harry Emerson Fosdick (1878–1968)

Chapter 3

✳ Now You Take the Survey

At the end of this chapter you'll find the survey questions that were used to obtain information for this book. Please answer the questions before going on to the next chapter.

If you want to find out what those things are that make that special person in your life feel precious and loved, don't just charge, in the way my friend Galen did, and get right into your partner's face and say, "Tell me five things that make you feel loved right now!" Error! Error! Schedule a quiet, appropriate time.

You should be prepared, yourself, by knowing those things that make you feel special or loved. You can use the information at the end of this chapter to prepare yourself.

Since women are more in touch with their feelings and emotions and tend to be more relational than men, they seem to have an easier time (usually at warp speed) describing what makes them feel loved. Men often take longer or present fewer things that make them feel special or loved. At the back of this book (Appendix A) are several pages for men and women containing responses from survey sheets collected from my speaking engagements. You can read them to see if you relate to what others have felt.

Once you know what makes that special person feel loved, you can open up a Love Bank Account and start making deposits.

Don't be too surprised if that person does not ask you what makes you feel loved. You see, you probably didn't know that person had a Love Bank to begin with. And if you didn't know that, you now have no idea about the status of the account. It might be in such disuse that it will take a little time to re-establish your credit or credibility so that the deposits will be accepted as genuine.

Try to come up with your own ideas first. If you have trouble, turn to the back of the book. Use a separate piece of paper if needed.

Now You Take The Survey

Please list on a separate sheet of paper those things that make you feel special or loved. (1-5)

How would you rate your marriage or current relationship on a scale of 1-10 (10 being a healthy, functioning relationship)?

Did your parents have a healthy, functioning relationship?

Using the above scale (1-10), how would you rate your parents' relationship?

In what areas was your family healthy or unhealthy?

Chapter 4

✳ Survey Results for Men and Women

Come on now, did you really do the survey?

At my speaking engagements, I have people fill out the survey that you just completed (you did fill it out, didn't you?) before we begin. As they complete their surveys, an interesting thing takes place. They turn the survey sheet over, fold it, or put it in a book. Heaven forbid that someone might see what makes them feel special and loved, especially someone who might be in a position of fulfilling those needs. The irony is, it's an open book test, folks.

Our survey forms are carbonless two copies; we keep one for our research and the participants keep one for sharing with a partner. It's interesting that we get back survey forms with little to nothing listed that makes the person feel special or loved, yet those people had high scores listed indicating that they had all come from healthy homes. I don't really think that you can get here from there.

During the presentation, I ask men if they know what the top two things are on women's survey forms that make them feel special or loved. They guess aimlessly.

Mike had just returned from his honeymoon. Since I know Mike pretty well, I took the liberty of asking him, "Now that you are married, do you know those things that will make your wife feel loved?" He also started guessing wildly. I shouldn't have been surprised, since I didn't know myself until I asked my wife after 22 years of marriage. I told Mike, "You just stood before God promising to honor and cherish your wife through sickness and health, until death do you part, and you don't have a clue as to what makes her feel loved." Mike said, "Well, why don't women tell us?"

Good point. But I already knew the other side of that equation from the women in my presentations. Without fail, what do you think women tell me when I ask them why they don't tell men what makes them feel loved? Answer, "If he really loved me, he would know." That's right. How does this work? These are not only unrealistic, but also unspoken expectations.

To Women: Let me, as Doctor Love, Ambassador of Good Will, tell you that we men will never know what it is that you want, need, and desire to make you know you are really loved. We don't have a sixth sense. We don't have, nor will we ever have, this tool. We aren't magicians. We can't pull the rabbit out of the hat on this one. **You must tell us**. Agreed? And you will probably have to tell us more than once. But you must tell us in such a way that we will understand it as much as we, as men, are able to. Then have us repeat what we heard. You might be surprised what you hear.

We were at the Wawona Hotel in Yosemite where we had met Jerry and his wife Bev. They were celebrating their 55th wedding anniversary. I asked Jerry if he knew those things that made his bride feel loved. He said in a gruff voice, "After 55 years I guess I do." His wife was sitting at an angle just behind him and she was rolling her eyes and shaking her head slowly and said, "He doesn't have a clue!."

The surveys only represent those who responded.

Nevertheless, what my surveys have shown from the beginning is that the results have been consistent for men and women. Most of those surveyed knew little or nothing about what made that other person in their relationship feel special or loved. The results didn't seem to have anything to do with age, nor with social, religious or economic conditions. This appears to be a universal problem.

There was a panel of women on a national television talk show who had been taken by con men, who had established relationships with them and sometimes married them. The methods these con artists had used were so similar that these women suspected that they had all been taken by the same man. Photos proved that they had not been. But the overwhelming reason these women gave as to why these guys were able to con their way into their lives was, "He listened to me!" This was the combination to the vault. This is the same combination for most women, according to our women's survey results. Written in many ways, the top two items that make women feel loved were, "He listens to me" and "He accepts and validates my feelings." Time after time, we were sure to find that these would be on most women's survey lists.

While doing a presentation for a men's retreat, a guy shared a story about what had happened to him two weeks before. His wife held a professional position. One particular night she had come home frazzled about something that had happened at work. He said that this was an unusual way for his wife to react. It was also unusual for him to do the following. He just sat there and listened for about 45 minutes. Just listened. One week later his wife was still thanking him for just listening. Do you think this was a big Love Bank deposit, friends? You bet. It was a huge deposit.

There was one thing that was noticeably missing from

women's survey lists that I thought would surely be there. What do you think it was? Right: **sex**. It's not that sex is not important to women. But when you ask women what makes them feel loved, they don't automatically think of sex.

All you really need to do here is focus on what women's interests are to understand them more. What kinds of magazines do women read? Usually not sex magazines. *Playgirl* went out of business. Women prefer those magazines that deal with home, family, fashion and career.

Eighty-three percent of the purchases made at malls are made by women. The stores know this. They also know that if a woman fails to make a purchase, she will go away feeling unfulfilled. Men are usually a ball and chain on women if they go shopping with them.

Men, on the other hand, only go shopping when they know exactly what they want and can find the parking space closest to the door of the store in which they want to make their purchase. The folks who run the mall also know this. As a result, those stores will try to stack up men's stuff by those entrances they know men might be prone to use in order to try to snag men for additional sales.

When we ask the women at our presentations what they think is on top of men's survey lists that make them feel loved, in chorus we often hear, "Sex."

Since sex is probably a "given" for most men, we will set that aside.

Then, ladies, what are the other top things that make men feel loved? This question usually produces the same type of aimless guessing that men make.

The real answers are, "Being supported in what we are doing" (i.e. job, hobby or other interest), and, this one gets us into big, big, big, big trouble, "Being accepted for where we are and not having to change." Most guys don't like to change. Change is inevitable if a relationship is going to mature. Women are usually programmed and ready to get on with it. This causes problems for men who list "being accepted for where we are and not having to change." Women are on this highway to intimacy. Most guys want to take the exit. They feel like women are trying to remake them into a Ken doll— to dress them and comb their hair and take them around to the other women showing how they have improved their man's life.

These are the top fifteen responses (in order of their priority) for men and women from the survey:

SURVEY RESULTS

MEN	WOMEN
Support (job, hobby, other interest)	Listening
Acceptance without change	Acceptance of Feelings
Nurturing	Togetherness
Hugs	Communication/ Conversation
Gifts	Hugs
Communication/Conversation	Thoughtfulness
Listening	Touching/Affection without sex
Attention	Respect
Touching	Support
Respect	Appreciation
Sex	Validation
Honesty	Attention
Encouragement	Cards, notes, surprises
Trust	Intimacy
Togetherness	Feeling/Being told, I Love You

These are the continuations of both lists in order of priority:

Men: Friendships, compliments, understanding, affirmation, appreciation, my own space, intimacy.

Women: Encouragement, compliments, nurturing,
            gifts, commitment, trust, invitations, honesty,
            phone calls.

Any surprises? As you can see, many of those things that make both men and women feel loved are on each others' lists, but at different levels. It appears that we all are wanting the same things, but we are trying to take different roads or using different methods to achieve our desires. It shouldn't make any difference how your responses match up to the survey. The important thing is to know what makes you personally feel special and loved.

It is really interesting that togetherness is near the top of the women's list, but at the bottom of the men's list. Men tend to be more distant in relational terms. But it becomes really clear here that in order to achieve those things that we all need to feel loved, there has to be togetherness.

Look how close together "hugs" are on both lists. Most of us need the constant reinforcement of being touched, hugged and held. Being this high on both lists at least shows the need and desire to be hugged.

We all have a *hug card* that enables us to get as many hugs as we want. But we aren't using the card enough. Check your hug card and see. Use the card often. And don't you ever think of coming up to hug me with one of those squeezes from the side and a phony kiss off into the air. If we are going to hug, we will hug in a frontal position. I'll ask first, of course. But you have to tell me how you like your hugs. Do you like a soft, medium or strong hug? Wait just a minute, where's my hug card?

So how do we make this work? Well, we're going to go on a little journey. We'll explore ideas and discover Nuggets of Life that have accumulated in my tool box, starting at a time when my own relationship was wobbling. It is the rebuilding of my relationship with my family through personal life experience, replacing the existing tools I had been given from an unhealthy home, as well as twelve years of research and experience gained from two start-up businesses, a loving 35-year marriage and further education that I want to share with you. You should have little trouble in identifying with me, in a humorous and practical way (you say you already have?) regarding the problems and common experiences we all encounter in our communication and relationships. Being able to acquire the Nuggets of Life can help you to regain the peace and happiness you are looking for. The opportunity is yours.

Don't try to use all the tools from this book at once. Try one tool that you can mutually agree upon to start things rolling. In a week or two, add another. Build on the successes as you use the tools.

So, here we go. Keep your hands and feet inside for the ride.

Chapter 5

✳ Transition to the Five-to-One Ratio

There is exciting relationship research coming from the Family Formation Project at the University of Washington in Seattle. John Gottman, Ph.D., an award-winning psychologist and author of *The Seven Principles for Making Marriage Work*, has conducted a twenty-six-year study on what makes love last. Dr. Gottman claims that there is no evidence that the theory of conventional counseling works. With up to 67% of marriages failing, and 50% of those couples who enter counseling still ending in divorce, one would expect the odds to be better if today's conventional counseling really was effective.

Dr. Gottman says, "Those who come to a therapist with an ailing marriage today can be like people going to a class to learn how to swim so they won't drown. But the instructors are armed only with a training program that teaches people how to do a triple flip off the high diving board or how to swim the English Channel." Not only doesn't today's therapy work, it's like going to a doctor for an illness and having him give you a treatment that makes your illness fatal.

What Dr. Gottman and his colleagues found is that couples who maintain a ratio of five positive moments (interactions) to each negative moment have relationships that last. Marriages that fall below a one-to-one ratio usually fail.

If your relationship experiences one of the following, is it doomed to fail?

1. Wildly explosive episodes, ranging from fierce arguments to intense making up.
2. A routine that is emotionally inexpressive.
3. A marriage in which the partners fight seldom or frequently.

Dr. Gottman believes that as long as the five-to-one ratio is in place, any marriage will work.

What is causing ripples in the counseling community is the fact that Dr. Gottman has discovered that volatile and conflict-avoiding marriages can be as stable as the marriages of traditional validating couples. The stability of these styles is determined by how each couple handles conflict.

Validating couples "compromise often, and calmly work out their problems to mutual satisfaction as they arise." They are viewed by counselors and friends as having the ideal marriage. Most counseling is directed toward getting couples to validate each other. The validating couple is like two therapists talking shop.

Volatile couples argue at the drop of the hat. They have emotional explosions and passionately romantic make-ups.

Conflict-avoiding couples will go to great lengths to keep the peace. They will minimize conflict by letting many problems go unresolved.

According to Dr. Gottman, the volatile and conflict-avoiding couples have just as much of a chance of making a go of their marriage as do the validating couples, as long as they maintain the five-to-one ratio. Often, couples who begin their marriages by complaining will end up having the most stable relationships. "In fact, trying to change the volatile and conflict-avoiding couples to become validating couples probably won't work," says Dr. Gottman.

A marriage can be more complicated where there are mixed styles, such as a volatile person who marries a conflict-avoiding person. Unless these different-styled people can settle on how they are going to resolve conflict, they will have difficulty in obtaining the vital five-to-one ratio.

It is important to have the "one" in the five-to-one ratio (to produce conflict and negativity). Dr. Gottman is convinced that the one negative experience is just as important as the five positive ones. "What may lead to temporary misery in a marriage, some disagreement and anger, may be healthier in the long run." Conflict can do good things. It can clear the air when pressures in the relationship get pent-up. It has functions of renewal and it also balances the relationship.

There are four negative acts that are more corrosive than others. They can predict failure. Dr. Gottman calls these "equestrians," the *four horsemen of the apocalypse*. They can take a marriage to hopelessness, despair and divorce. The four horsemen are criticism, defensiveness, contempt and stonewalling.

The lead horseman is criticism. Gottman says, "The difference between complaint and criticism is that criticism has blaming in it. It's attacking someone else's personality or character, instead of being specific about a complaint."

The second horseman is defensiveness. Criticism is more likely to create defensiveness in someone. It becomes more personal. It's perceived as more of an attack. A person will try to defend himself or herself by denying responsibility and dishing back calculated insults. A couple can drop right into defensiveness without passing "go" by being too sensitive to legitimate complaints.

The third horseman is contempt. Dr. Gottman says, "What separates contempt from criticism is the intent to insult and psychologically abuse your partner. Contempt is the acid in the relationship." Putting down your partner with insulting jokes, critical comments, facial expressions and verbal abuse can destroy any chance of intimacy. Men who are negative and contemptuous can make women physically ill.

All hope is abandoned when the last horseman, stonewalling, is saddled up and sent from the starting gate. Stonewallers withdraw from interacting emotionally in the marriage. They just stop communicating, even if an insulting situation occurs. Eighty-five percent of stonewallers are men. This might be an evolutionary survival technique.

All of the four horsemen occasionally ride through most relationships. Breaking the corrosive cycles by repair intervention prevents the marriage from falling into what Gottman calls "the distance and isolation cascade." This cascading usually propels negative thoughts and situations that lead to separation and divorce. At this stage people believe they can't work out their problems. They separate themselves from each other in living and all activities, electing to solve their problems outside the relationship. There is a dramatic change in perception in how they see the positive and negative behavior of the other partner.

They feel low and have crummy thoughts. Once this threshold has been crossed, it's hard to make the transition back. The body takes on a change in how it now perceives what is going on in the relationship. This can involve a situation called flooding.

Dr. Gottman refers to flooding as when "you feel overwhelmed and disorganized by the way your partner expresses negativity. Couples can feel flooded by one another by the ways they express complaints. They get hypervigilant about negative things. The body of someone who feels flooded is a confused jumble of signals. It may be hard to breathe. Muscles tense and stay tensed. The heart beats fast and seems to beat harder."

Once the heart rate reaches 95-100 beats per minute, the adrenal glands go into action delivering adrenaline. This excited state interferes with the listening and other understanding skills needed to do the necessary repair work in the relationship.

Dr. Gottman believes that repair attempts are a way to break the cycle of the four horsemen. This involves talking about how you are communicating. It requires making statements such as, "Can we please stay on the subject?" "That was a rude thing to say." "I don't think you're listening to me." In bad and stable relationships, learning to accept (instead of ignore) and use the repair attempts is critical, even when they are presented in a heated emotional conflict. It can help couples when they mess up and start mounting up and riding with the posse of the four horsemen. This repair work is an interaction that pulls on the reins to prevent a stampede of negativity. It's a form of transition from mostly negative moments to a healthier way of resolving conflict in order to achieve the five-to-one ratio.

Gottman's Keys to Happiness

Dr. Gottman believes there are four simple keys to creating happier relationships:

1. Learn how to calm down. Little or no effective communication or counseling is going to be heard once "flooding" takes place. Once a couple can start

calming down, both partners will have a chance to work on the other three keys.

2. Learn to listen and speak non-defensively. Being able to re-channel the destructive habit of defensiveness is one of the most valuable transitions you can make. Replacing defensiveness with listening, and then speaking without affixing blame can help "reintroduce praise and admiration into your relationship."

3. Validate your partner. We already know from surveys that validation of one another is one of the most important factors in making your partner feel loved. Validation involves "putting yourself in your partner's shoes and imagining his or her emotional state." Listening, accepting and validating your partner's feelings, even if you have to say you are struggling to try to understand, all greatly advance the repairing of a relationship; this is especially true when they are coupled with accepting responsibility, apologizing when one is wrong, and accepting and validating the partner's point of view.

4. Practice. Dr. Gottman refers to this "over learning" as practicing to the point where you automatically calm down, communicate non-defensively, and validate your partner even when the "spit hits the fan."

Chapter 6

✳ How Does This All Work for Me?

What's exciting for me is that I believe the Love Bank I have described is an accounting system for Dr. Gottman's five-to-one ratio. Imagine what could happen if you used this information. Suppose you opened a Love Bank Account with that special person in your life and used it to transcend to the five-to-one ratio.

Well, go back with me a few months ago when I was working at the firehouse. Paul was called in to work for four hours of overtime. He was from a different station and shift. Knowing I had done some communication and relationship work, he took me aside and said, "Bob, I'm in big trouble." I asked, "With what?" He said, "My marriage! I don't know what I'm going to do."

Paul said that he got no support from the guys at the firehouse. He explained, "When I try to tell them what is going on, they hit me in the chest and say, 'Forget her, let's go get hammered.'"

Paul told me that six months earlier he and his wife had what I call **"the talk."** The talk can come whenever situations build up and aren't resolved. It usually blindsides one of the partners. Paul's wife told him he wasn't part of her life. He was always gone with the guys, coaching and/or competing in sports, besides working his firefighter shifts. She didn't think he loved her anymore, and she was losing her love for him, too.

Like most guys, firefighters get many of their needs met at work. We have certainty, uncertainty, variety, significance, discipline, comfort, connection, growth and contribution. Because we go home with our tank pretty full, we aren't always motivated to provide the same vital necessities for our partners.

Paul attempted to make changes. But he made the **big** mistake of not asking his wife what changes she wanted. And if the changes aren't what the other person needs, it doesn't make any difference what a person does.

So now it was six months later and she still felt the same way. She threatened to leave with their four-year-old son. She stated that because of what had already happened, counseling was not an option.

From our conversation, I suspected that Paul's wife, Tara, was at Dr. Gottman's level four, stonewalling. Had she crossed the line?

I sent Paul home with four chapters from this book. As Tara read the chapter on the five-to-one ratio, she said, "I'm right here," pointing to stonewalling. Had she crossed the line? Reading the other chapters, she said, "Did he write this about you? Because this is exactly what you've been doing."

They went for a walk and discussed the chapters. They talked several times during the next three days. Then Tara caught some hope. Maybe with these new tools, they could work it out. Paul took the time to ask Tara the changes she really needed. He opened a Love Bank Account and started making deposits. He started his transition toward the five-to-one ratio.

🔥   *Hope is the anchor for the soul.*

Three weeks later she felt it was real; Paul wasn't just putting out spot fires, as before. Tara said, "I think I still love you." Three months later they went away to celebrate their anniversary. I saw Paul a month later and he said, "It's never been better."

One year later he told me, "It's still hard work, but well worth it. It's never like before because we have the Nuggets of Life needed to work it out."

This firefighter became a hero in his own home by saving his marriage. Imagine what could happen in your life?

Nugget: Open a Love Bank Account. Use it as an accounting system to transition to the five-to-one ratio.

How: Make the kinds of deposits your partner needs most.

Testimonial from Paul

Two years ago was a terrible year for my family; or so I thought. Actually, my five-year marriage was not as great as I assumed. It all came down on top of me that summer.

Two things happened in our marriage relationship that made me realize something was wrong. First, my wife spent more time and seemed to have more fun with her friends than with me. And second, we hardly ever communicated or did things together. When we did, it was not fun. We had grown apart.

My wife told me that she no longer loved me and I was in danger of losing her to someone else! If I did not become a better husband, father, *listener* and friend, she was planning on moving out. I was shocked, amazed, hurt and disappointed, but she was right in every way. I did not know who to turn to. I was embarrassed to tell anyone about my problems.

One day while working with Captain Bob, we had a discussion about women. My problems with communicating and listening to my wife surfaced. With Bob's words of wisdom, and passages and excepts from his book, my wife and I were able to identify the problems in all facets of our relationship. We have become best friends again, and now I can honestly say that we are on the road to salvaging our marriage. It is a continuing process! We must work at it each day.

I realized one thing through this whole ordeal. We both need each other a lot, and if we know how to listen and can communicate better with each other, the better our relationship will be in the long run.

 Being in love *means speaking the same language.*
Loving means speaking the other person's language.
—The Rt. Rev. John R. Wyatt

Chapter Seven

A Broadway Play

Chapters seven through eighteen provide tools/skills for a side drawer in your tool box. Use these Nuggets of Life (tools/skills) to enable others to let you know what they need from you and to help you receive what you need from them.

A Broadway play doesn't start on Broadway. It starts on the road, where the performers can work out the bugs in the script and refine the play until it's ready for the bright lights of Broadway.

If you don't already have the following Nuggets in your tool box, you'll need a time "on the road" with your partner, where you can try them out to see what "plays" and what doesn't. Expect to feel uncomfortable if you have never used these Nuggets before. It's normal for you to experience a little stage fright at first. That's okay. Before long you'll become comfortable with your new role. And once you are, go for the bright lights of Broadway.

Chapter Eight

Give Clear and Direct Signals

Most people respond to our needs by what we tell them. If we aren't truthful about our needs, others are responding to the wrong information. People can't guess what we need. We need to give them clear and direct signals as to what we want. You make an effort to adjust your behavior when someone tells you clearly what he or she needs, don't you? Well, other folks are willing to be equally accommodating most of the time.

We can't do this by sending coded messages or trying to ricochet them around the room or through others, hoping they will get it by osmosis, or by dropping hints that you are sure they will understand. You must open that little slot between your nose and your chin and say it.

We miss great opportunities to communicate by not telling people what we really want and need from them. We should also encourage others to give *us* clear and direct signals so that we will really know what they need from us. According to James Patterson, co-author of *The Day America Told the Truth*, 81% of all Americans lie about their feelings. He remarks, "People say what they think others want to hear." According to the survey, 91% of people in the U.S. say they lie routinely, and 36% confess to dark important lies. Americans lie at the drop of a hat about everything from whether or not they really love their spouse (29% say they're not sure) to the quality of food when they're dining out.

You know, those folks at the restaurant really do want to know if everything is okay with our meal. I just wish they wouldn't come by our table on a programmed basis and say, "Is everything okay?" Everyone with big smiles responds, "Oh, yes," when it might not be true. If the meal is not okay, they want to make it right, or steer someone else away from what you didn't care for, or bring you something else. They would rather make it right instead of possibly losing a valued customer. They really want to be told the truth.

Other statistics found in the survey include the following:

- 86% of the people surveyed lie regularly to parents; 75% to friends; 73% to children; and 69% to spouses.
- 43% lie about income; 40% about sex.
- 51% said there is no reason to marry; 31% are having an extramarital affair.

Wow! How can we expect things to change when up to 81% of our lives is made up of lies about our feelings.

Why do people do this? It's usually based on fear.

Are you a member of this fraternity? Are you afraid that if you tell people how you really feel, they will go away not liking you? Do you need their approval? What you might find out when you start giving clear and direct signals is that people don't go away, they actually come closer because they then know how you really feel. And although it can be uncomfortable at first (you have seldom done it before), it is a great feeling to watch others adjust to what you really need.

🔥   *Water a drop at a time will eventually float a whale.*

There are three ways to accomplish the goal of giving clear and direct signals:

(1) passively, (2) assertively, or (3) aggressively. We don't want anyone going on a suicide mission. The best overall results will come from being clearly assertive. If you find yourself uncomfortable about a situation with a sinking feeling in the pit of your stomach (your stomach is the sounding board of your emotions), don't overreact. Don't let the pendulum of your emotions take a wild swing. Just formulate what you want to say as clearly and briefly as possible so it can be understood by the person you are telling it to. Use K.I.S.S. to deliver your message. (Keep It Simple, Sweetie.) Please don't dredge up all the past hurts and try to club the other person over the head. You haven't told this person along the way how you really feel, so don't try to make up for the lost opportunities.

Say what you need to say . . . then shut up. And stay quiet. You have placed the ball in the other person's court. Let that person field it. Don't try to figure out what the other person is thinking. You won't be able to. Besides, if you don't shut up, you might end up saying something silly or stupid that will weaken your previous statement. You might try to minimize, water down, or say, "Oh, well, it's not really that important" or "It's really no big deal," when really it is. If you have to say anything (try not to), be the broken record and repeat only what you have already said (this is great for kids) once, twice, three times or more.

There are some people who have no problem expressing, telling and forcing their views on others. They feel that they have been blessed with the gift of criticism. They are always angry at life. They would complain if they were lynched by a posse and not hung with a new rope. Acting like these folks will cause you to lose relationships and jobs. Know your motivation. Use this tool only to change the things you need to be living healthier.

🔥   *Unasked for advice is still criticism.*

Let me give you an example of what I'm talking about when I refer to giving clear and direct signals. I had a new fire station assignment and the guys there liked Health Nut bread for meals. I love multi-grain breads, but I don't care for Health Nut bread. Well, it's no big deal, right? Wrong. If I didn't say I didn't like the bread, I would be eating Health Nut bread until I retire. So, I told them I didn't care for the bread. They adjusted and bought another bread. Whole wheat bread. There is only one bread I don't like even more than Health Nut bread and that is whole wheat bread. But, since I didn't give a clear signal that I really liked Honey Wheat Berry bread, how could they know? Once I told them my preference, they adjusted. I did, too. We tried to keep their bread *and* my bread on hand.

Another time, I made reservations at Strizzi's restaurant and requested table 32. Table 32 is in a corner where you can people-watch (you like to do that, too, huh?). When we arrived at the restaurant on time we saw people being seated at table 32. In the past I would have folded and said "no big deal." This was our favorite table. I first asked (a good idea before you embarrass yourself) if we hadn't reserved the table. We had. Then why (a clear and direct signal) was my table given away (assertive—ball in his court)? Embarrassment, confusion, apologies and then the offer of another table. The apology was all that was needed.

Now they wanted to buy us dessert. We didn't want dessert that night, so we passed. In the mail came a note for a complimentary dessert next time we were in. The next time I called they said, "Oh, Mr. Smith, you want table 32, don't you?" Well, yes. I had forgotten the note about the free dessert, but they hadn't. One night when we had a reservation to be at table 32 at 6:15 p.m. (this is really a neat place to eat, close to our home) Harriet was delayed. I called to inform them we wouldn't be in until 7:00 p.m., I told them I understood if they couldn't hold our table. When we arrived at 7:00 p.m. there were people waiting to get in from out front. The restaurant was full. Except for table 32. They had kept our table open. A feeling of validation? You bet. Humbling, too.

Nugget: If you want things to change, give a clear and direct signal of what you need to have happen. Don't be part of the 81% who lie about their feelings. Be the broken record.

How: Think about what you need to say and deliver it in a clear assertive way. Don't be passive or aggressive. If you need to, start with small things. You do know what kind of bread you like, don't you? Once you're on a roll, you'll get better at putting the signal out.

Chapter Nine

Don't Take the Bait
(Somebody Else Might Want to Eat It)

What's the bait? It's anything or any situation that would lure you in and then push your buttons. Taking the bait is a subtle act of being snagged. Like any good bait for a fish, it will come disguised in many forms. Once you have taken the bait, the person who enticed you will set the hook. Then, you'll be hooked into the trap of using the old behavior that makes you crazier than usual.

Who tries to get you to take the bait? Parents, partners, spouses, kids, employers and employees, even siblings. Now that you know what the bait is and who presents it, think of the times recently when you took it. Who tried to get you to take the bait? Can you refuse it next time?

Once you are aware of what the bait is, you won't have to take it. You don't have to respond, or you can simply say, "You're probably right," or "No!" or "Stop!" and swim away. You could ask, "Why are you telling me this?" Or say, "No, I really don't want to know this information."

This tool alone will save you much anguish.

Nugget: Don't take the bait.

How: Recognize the trap, choose not to fall into it, and swim on to better things.

🔥   *My mother was a travel agent for guilt trips.*

Chapter Ten

Stop Holding

Are you ever in situations in which someone says something that angers or bothers you and what is said causes a feeling of pressure in your chest and stomach? Do you grit your teeth, and unconsciously hold your breath to maintain your cool exterior and just remain quiet? This is holding. It's when you internalize the situation instead of expressing how you feel. Many people think this is the way to prevent conflict, to keep everything smooth, and not to rock the boat or ruffle anyone's feathers.

But what happens to you once these situations develop? Does holding them inside help you solve your grievances? No, they really don't go away. And they *will* find their way out if you don't respond and you continue to hold your feelings inside. They will manifest themselves as stress, tension, ulcers, anxiety attacks, overeating, headaches, stomach and back pain, sleep disorders, diarrhea, depression, colitis, and a multitude of other ailments. You can break this habit of holding. This next chapter will show you how.

🔥 *Doubt your doubts.*

Chapter Eleven

Practice Present-Moment Living

Whenever you feel you are holding and not expressing an emotional reaction you are feeling, you should attempt to respond right then. This is present-moment living. It's expressing yourself whenever the situation happens. You don't have to do it in a vicious or aggressive way, but you do have to transmit a clear and direct signal that states how you really feel. It's important that you release all the feelings you are holding.

Yes, this could be confrontational to some people. (You know, there are some people around us who never have ulcers. They're just carriers.)

But you will be surprised how easy present-moment living becomes with practice. You can become a healthier person because of the honest responses you give when negative situations occur.

Remember, a whine is a scream through a small opening.

Chapter Twelve

Set Healthy Boundaries

By giving clear and direct signals and using present-moment living, you are setting healthy boundaries. Setting a boundary is simply the act of training others how you want to be treated. A quick example of a boundary setting can be seen when someone walks so near to you, you feel his presence from the front or back. If anyone moves too close within your physical territory, you feel uncomfortable and probably will move away from that person in order to re-establish your boundary. Boundaries are set at different distances for different people. For some, the boundary is too close when a certain person just enters the room.

Without boundaries in your life, you have no defenses to prevent others from intruding on your very existence. A lack of boundaries creates chaos with your time, finances and virtually every other aspect of your life.

Setting healthy boundaries is part of identifying who you really are. It is like stepping on the brake pedal to flash your brake lights to someone following too closely behind your car. It's a warning that the other person is inside your safety zone.

A boundary is that point at which someone else's territory ends and yours begins. Some of us have well-established personal boundary lines that set us apart from others, whereas others have only a few. The latter people don't know how to say "no" to almost any request. As such, other people have access to them 24 hours a day under any circumstances. They could be bleeding to death inside, but they can't bring themselves to exercise their "no" reflex when they are asked to do something. They hate themselves afterward for accepting another thing they don't have time for. They are in shock, feel guilty and are ashamed of taking on what they probably can't handle. The old adage "if you want something done, give it to a busy person" doesn't apply here. If I feel that if I don't do it, it won't get done or if I act as if everyone else's needs take priority over mine, then my helping you usually ends up hurting me.

We only need to realize that personal identity is built on personal choices and by setting one's own limits. It requires stopping our habit of taking on too much responsibility for other people's work, obligations and needs. *Everyone* has needs.

You can start by establishing small territories at first. As you succeed at this, you can extend your property lines. The next time someone asks you to do something, check your comfort level. If it doesn't feel right, set your boundary at a point where it fits your comfort level. If you don't want to do what is requested, a simple "thanks for thinking of me but I already have other plans" is a polite way of saying **"no."** Then, be quiet. No other explanation is needed. You might be surprised to find out that other people can be comfortable with your boundary (decision).

If you only knew how seldom people worry about what *you* think *they* are thinking about *you*, your anxiety level would decrease tremendously.

We can't expect always to be able to say "no" to everything we don't want to do. It's being able to say "yes" to the appropriate situations that enables us to grow into people who know how to set healthy limits.

Setting healthy boundaries also involves letting people help us. There are those who would do almost anything to help a friend or even someone they don't know. However, when they need help, they would rather go below and fall on their sword than allow or ask someone else to provide help. When asked, "How are you doing?" they would answer, "Oh, we're just fine over here," although they could be dying by degrees. Just remember the next time someone says, "Oh, we're just fine over here," that the initials F.I.N.E. stand for Fearful, Insecure, Neurotic, and Emotional.

By taking on every project in sight, becoming overloaded, and not allowing others to assist and help you (especially if you're the one who needs help), you rob people of the opportunity and satisfaction of being involved in your projects and possibly of paying you back for your kindness.

> **Nugget:** Exercise your "no" reflex to establish healthy boundaries to your comfort level. Your body will give you a signal that when you are saying "yes" you really mean **"no!"**
>
> **How:** Be honest. Set limits. Be persistent. Step back and let others help.

Personal Experience by Linda

My life was a wreck but I didn't know why. Then I started a 12-step program. I was asked at one of the meetings to list all the things I was involved in. Once I wrote them down, I couldn't believe I was trying to take care of all those things. I found out that I just couldn't say **"no!"** I borrowed the tool of saying, "Thanks for thinking about me, but I already have other plans," to try to get my life in order.

The person who loaned me the tool called me two days later pretending to need some typing done right away. I used the tool. But he wasn't the first one I had used it on. The day after my meeting, I was called to head a decorating committee. "Thanks, I already have other plans."

And the following day a friend called and wanted me to go shopping. My body told me I didn't want to go. My friend was comfortable with my decision. She just said, "Maybe next time." I was able to say "no," maybe for the first time. Being able to say "no" freed my life. I was not only able to say no, but also to feel good about it.

I still fail at times. But the difference is I now know when it's happening and I remember that particular meeting and the tool I received. For the last three years I have been involved in women's events at our church. This is a healthy choice for me which allows me to feel validated and to receive satisfaction. This has really taught me how to let others use their gifts and talents instead of taking everything on myself. I'm now working on organizing an area women's retreat.

Where I used to try to do everything myself, there now are fifteen ladies participating. One lady came to her first retreat two years ago. She is now working on this year's planning committee. To see her so excited about being a part of this year's retreat is a joy that is hard to put into words. Right now, just putting all this down on paper reminds me of what I have accomplished. It makes my heart sing praises to God.

Chapter Thirteen

Where Are You on Your Own Personal Agenda?

Simply put, on a scale from 1 to 10 (10 being the highest) where are you on your own personal agenda? When I was first asked this question, I knew right away that I was between a #4 and #5. In other words, there were as many as five things at that time that were preoccupying my life and keeping me from being #10 on my own personal agenda—and preventing me from enjoying life more and achieving personal peace and happiness.

What was most disturbing was that I was always at #5, #4, #3 or less; never #9 or #10. I was out of control, spending a lot of wasted time and energy being focused on, obsessed with and overly responsible for others, trying to control everything within my reach, and ending up being the miserable victim in the end. Isn't it interesting that when we're so busy trying to fix and help others we don't have time to feel the pain of our own problems? Some people work really hard at not being happy. Happiness is a choice!

We have been taught that we should put others first and be all things to other people. I believe we can't begin to help others in a healthy way until we are healthy. If there is an emergency on an airliner, the instructions are to put your oxygen mask on first before helping others. How can we expect to be in this position unless we have good self-esteem, healthy energy (not a compulsive controlling drive), balance, and adequate rest to draw from? These things can happen if you position yourself in a healthy way at the top of your own personal agenda.

I started to move up in importance on my own agenda only when I started practicing "detaching." Each time I was tempted to get involved in weeding other people's gardens or getting into their bubble with things that were none of my business, I would try to "detach" from the situation.

You know, there are some people who we encounter in life (including family members) who have such overwhelming needs we could never do enough to fulfill them. They have that ability to hook us in and suck out our energy. All too often we become the unhealthy friend/counselor. We don't have the tools to begin to fix these people nor does anyone else for that matter. It's tough enough to try to fix ourselves! In the process of trying to fix and rescue others, these people usually end up resenting our attempts and we become the victims (again). You cannot make people happy anyway; you can only participate in their happiness.

By the way, do you know how it is that our parents know how and where to push our hot buttons? They installed them.

Being able to detach can be a huge step toward rebuilding your self image. This skill alone can mean a new beginning in your life. Detachment is simply the ability to live your own life. It isn't living a life that is centered on or reacting to someone else. Detachment is a tool needed by those who have been damaged by an unhealthy family life, but it doesn't come easily or quickly. For me it was a constant struggle. Whenever someone would come up to me with a problem or crisis, I would get hooked right back into the old pattern of going to the wall to risk all in order to rescue someone and thereby get my adrenaline started.

To keep myself from playing Superman, I started carrying a 3 x 5 card that had written across the front, **Stop—Detach— Why are you doing this? This is a trap. You have been here before.**

Stopping did not come easily. With much practice it finally did happen. I was able to stop; I was able to stop the mouse from running around inside my head. Detachment was an essential ingredient for any hope of future happiness.

Without the ability to detach, the anxiety will become progressively worse, not better. Miracles happen, but they are infrequent. There is a great incentive here once you learn the art and acquire the tool of detachment. You will experience increased energy both physically and mentally as you learn not to worry about things and people you have no control over. This is taking care of yourself.

Detachment can restore you to healthy thinking and make you free to be responsible for yourself, not for others, and to fulfill the needs on your own personal agenda. Aren't you tired by now of doing things the wrong way? This is not to say that we will or should always be at the top of our agenda everyday. That is not realistic. There will be situations that demand your complete attention and those upper positions for a short time. But it should be an objective to know where you are now on your own agenda and to work toward the healthy balanced upper end.

   We can't control the direction of the wind, but we can adjust our sails.

If you say that you have been plagued by this ailment but that you now have it under control, then why do you still keep an inventory on everything and everyone around you? **Detach!**

Where are you on your own personal agenda?

Nugget: Be able to detach from becoming centered on, reacting to, focusing on, or overly responsible for others. Let people be responsible for themselves.

How: Practice hard to live your own life in a balanced way so that you will move up on your own personal agenda. Weed your own garden, and stay in your own bubble.

Personal Experience by Chris

I have really benefited from detaching! Have you ever sat down to a nice hot meal when you were really hungry? Right away you take a big bite only to find out it's too hot for your mouth. You want to spit it out, but you're afraid it would look bad in front of others. So, you just let it burn your mouth. That's what it felt like to me trying to be a problem-solver instead of learning to detach. I was carrying around this burning feeling in my gut, seeking approval from those around me.

What I've learned from detaching is that I couldn't solve other people's problems and that I was trying to seek approval from others for my own self-esteem.

Detaching has made me feel better about myself. I have more control emotionally. I have become closer to my family. Funny isn't it—I had to detach to become closer. In the process, I gained the respect and approval from the others

around me that I was so desperately trying to obtain.
            Detach,

                        Detach,

                                    Detach.

    Chris told me later that while writing out his experience he realized what he had accomplished. He felt that he had established deeper roots with his family and other folks around him.

Chapter Fourteen

What Does That Mean?

We can't always know what other people mean when they say something, because we all come from such varied backgrounds and lifestyles. Sometimes we even speak different dialects (especially men and women). Whenever you are in the slightest doubt, ask the question, "What does that mean?" Instead of speculating about what the person meant and projecting the statement way down the road, this simple question will eliminate the confusion, holding, loss of sleep, fear and worry.

You will probably find that by asking the question you will seldom be close to being right about what you think the response is.

> *Feelings are chemical and can kill or cure.*
> **—Bernie S. Siegle, M.D.**

Chapter Fifteen

What Do You Want to See Happen?

Problems are inevitable, misery is optional. Problems will come. It's how we process and deal with them that can make the difference. The composer Irving Berlin said, "Life is 10% of how you make it and 90% of how you take it."

All too often, people focus so intensely on problems, feeding themselves with anxiety and fear (fear is the place where negative thoughts are developed), they seldom have a clear idea as to what they want to see happen.

People sometimes come up to me after a speaking engagement wanting to pour out a huge problem. Finally, they think, someone will understand their situation. I actively listen. (I attempt to direct them to some qualified person with the staff from the sponsoring organization for assistance.) I do ask them, though, what they want to see happen. This often stops them dead in their tracks. They are usually so overwhelmed with the problem, they haven't given the solution much thought. Once they stop focusing on the problem and start focusing on their resources and options, and get a plan, the fear and anxiety levels drop on the intensity scale. Now they can redirect their focus to reality and a possible solution.

One cannot get through life without pain . . . what we can do is choose how to use the pain life presents to us.
—Bernie S. Siegel, M.D.

Personal Experience by Ayn

A near-perfect vacation experience was fast coming to an abrupt halt. The cloud-strewn sky that stood as a backdrop for Flat Iron Ridge, which I daily admired, would be a hazy memory, even hard to recall once I returned home to "my problem."

The peace, tranquillity and deep serenity of my feelings would disappear, giving way to painful memories if I allowed myself to even lightly dwell on matters left at home. What I was returning to was a painful experience with a woman whom I thought was a good friend. I felt betrayed by her shoddy treatment of both my daughter and me. Her behavior toward us was unkind, almost callous. In its wake were my feelings of betrayal, frustration and deep rage.

As I realized that vacations do not last forever and that eventually you do have to "come home," I let the painful memories and feelings surface. I recounted the events that led to the estrangement of my friend and me to some other friends. They could see by my furrowed brow, tight lips and the pinched expression on my face that my serenity was fast disappearing. As I continued to recount each incident—one more insulting than the next—I felt hot stinging tears, dammed up, just waiting to erupt.

I was working myself into a fevered state. My friends listened intently, their eyes never leaving my face, punctuated with sympathetic nods and expressions of understanding and compassion. Then, suddenly, they stopped my tale of woe and asked, "What do you want from this woman?"

The question took me by complete surprise, but after a few moments of racing thoughts my mind settled on the one answer that fit best.

I responded, "An apology. I want her to say that she is sorry for hurting us."

My friends' response was, "Is she capable of that?"

That question was the most surprising of all. I had never viewed it from that angle. I had assumed that she was laden with abilities and spiritual awareness.

As I examined our relationship more carefully, I began to see the cracks—the tiny hairline fractures that seemed to run through this woman's personality.

"No, she is not capable of that." As I said it, I realized that it was, in fact, true. I was hoping for something she was not capable of giving. I had not realized her limitations before.

Feelings of relief and peace followed. I felt as if a huge boulder had been lifted from my back and I could breathe again. Relief flooded into me. That simple but profound realization let me out of my prison cell of grief. I had felt my feelings, mourned them and was ready for the funeral to be over.

🔥   *The solution is there, you just haven't seen it yet.*

Chapter Sixteen

How Can I Stop Using Worst-Case Scenarios?

Worry is interest on a debt you may not owe.

If a problem arises, often the following procedure offers a routine course of action:

1. A problem is perceived on the horizon.
2. You consider the resources available to you and can usually resolve the problem at this level.
3. If not, you pull out all the stops, call 911, hit Code 3, and go to general quarters. In other words, you respond as though this is a worst-case scenario.

Whereas steps one and two are pretty common and should solve most situations, there is seldom the need for step three to even be. We should be able to use rational thought, honesty, logic and determination to solve problems. Often, however, many of us don't. As soon as step one appears on the horizon, we bypass step two and go immediately to step three. This is a worst-case scenario.

We waste huge amounts of energy worrying about every perceived problem. Often it becomes such a habit, we just attach our free-floating anxieties to any possible problem that comes remotely close to us and we make it into a worst-case scenario. I knew someone who did this all too well. My mother was a world class worrier. If there was a plane crash anywhere on the planet when my family and I were on vacation, she somehow believed we were probably on it. Unfortunately, people can become worriers just by being around people like my mother.

Mark Twain wrote, "I have known a great many troubles. Most of them never happened." I now keep this motto over my desk. I was able to break the habit of worrying by keeping a log of perceived problems on a 5x8 yellow tablet with the following information:

Date _____

- What is the problem?
- What do you think is going to happen?
- What would you like to see happen?
- Since prayer is the place where burdens change shoulders, this is an appropriate place for a prayer. It can release your perceived burden to the power of the universe.

Then stop yourself in this process and ask this question. What is the worst thing that could happen? If this did happen, could you live with it? **Yes** or **No**? In most situations just knowing you can live with the worst situation, if it really happened, releases the paralyzing hold on you.

Dr. Norman Vincent Peale wrote about Jim Johnson, a friend from New York, who said during a huge storm, "No matter how large and dark the clouds get, or how much rain, lightning and thunder, **I never knew a storm that didn't blow itself out**." It can be the same with our perceived problems. They will eventually blow over.

Once your problem situation passes, go back to your tablet and add in this information:

Today's Date _____

What actually happened? _____

You might be as shocked as I was. After almost two tablets of situations, none of the perceived problems turned out the way I had envisioned they would. **None!**

 If you expect the best, you are given some strange kind of power to create conditions that produce the desired results.

By being able to go back over page after page of wrong reactions, I was able to break the cycle and change the manner in which I processed potential problems. But really this had more to do with processing life itself.

Fear knocked at the door.

Faith answered.

No one was there.

 Bacteria and other microorganisms find it easier to infect people who worry and fret.
—Leo Rangdell

Chapter Seventeen

Change Brings Change
(Sometimes with Pain)

We waste huge amounts of time trying to change (or fix) other people. How can we ever expect to change someone else when it is so difficult to change ourselves?

Think about it. When change comes into your life (at work or home), the RCs go up (resistance to change); this is especially true if the change directly affects you and you had no input on what has happened. Big RCs.

In order to initiate change, you need the help of the only person who can help you: yourself. That's right. By first accepting and taking the responsibility for where you are (instead of blaming others) and by working on yourself for your own peace, happiness and mental health, you'll be able to make significant changes.

> 🔥 *Look in the mirror instead of the magnifying glass.*

As you change, those around you will probably change also (if they are capable of change at all). If they don't, you can still be a happier, healthier, and more peaceful person. If this is rocking the boat, well, so be it. In fact, you might need to capsize that boat in order to cause the necessary changes.

You might think you are changing people, but you are probably only taking hostages (or making yourself the hostage). Some people will lead you to believe (trick you into thinking) that they are changing just long enough to get you to back off; then they will get you back on the merry-go-round for another ride with their former behavior. Let's check your merry-go-round ride card. My, my, you have been on a lot of rides, haven't you? Isn't it time to step off the ride?

 Most people don't change because they see the light. They usually feel the heat!

It's nearly impossible to change other people. You *can* change yourself however, and that's a big enough job in itself. Change takes hard work. Maybe that's why so many people don't attempt change. If you know of any way to make change come easily, I'm really interested in hearing from you. You can call collect.

One of the reasons people fail at change is that it causes chaos. In that chaos they are often worn down and forced back to the status quo. What they don't realize is chaos is normal with change. You must go through chaos before you can achieve new behavior. Hang in there just a little longer. Studies have shown that people who set a goal to change a behavior and failed quit after seven days. They probably were not aware that behavior changes start becoming permanent after the twenty-first day.

 The will of God will never place you where the grace of God can't help you.

Some people use passive aggressive behavior when you attempt to change them. They say to your face what you want to hear but they have no intention of doing it. It's like a big dog licking your face and wetting on your leg at the same time.

Men and women can be double-talkers. You've seen them. You might have been or currently are one; you know, one of those couples who are fighting already and they aren't even married yet. They think things will be different once they get married. As many of you already know, it doesn't get any better than it was before you were married. Those problems won't go away easily, if at all (unless you have Dr. Gottman's five-to-one ratio). Then, after they're married, couples think if they have a baby all their problems will be solved. Right? Wrong! This lovable bundle of joy (the enemy) will only compound the problems, and add new ones. Then the couple believes the answer is a new house, car, boat, or they use a geographical fix by moving to a new area. Really? Not likely. Those *things* will just put those problems on hold for awhile. I guarantee you they'll be back. They never leave, actually.

People seem to change only when there is enough pain; pain in the form of the loss of a job, family or health. How often do you see someone trying to change when things are going great for them? There is seldom a reason. **Success is a great deodorant**. If your changing causes another person enough pain, he or she might also change. There are no guarantees, however.

When you initiate change you might be quickly referred to as the *identified problem* as to why things aren't working. Another person may have no clue as to why you are attending those meetings or reading those books; they say it is all a bunch of crap. You can't touch one part of a mobile without it affecting the rest of its parts.

So if you can't fix others, can you make other people happy? You can only participate. Unfortunately, there are some people who work, unconsciously, really hard at not being happy.

It's been said that if you tried to place a frog in hot water, he will instantly jump out. Take that same frog and put it in a pan of cold water on a stove. Turn on the heat. The water will come to a boil and the frog will die without making an attempt to jump. Familiar?

Nugget: Only changed people change people. The only proven way to change others is to first change yourself. If the other person doesn't change, at least you will be living a healthier, more peaceful life. Get healthy yourself and set an example, particularly for your children.

How: Persistence. Educate yourself by reading the abundance of available material and by joining support groups in your town. If you become overwhelmed, seek professional guidance. Don't relapse.

Personal Experience by Judy

I was always buying books trying to find ways to fix and change my husband. I stopped. It didn't work. I took the focus off my husband and started working on myself. I started by concentrating on educating myself. With books, support groups and doing those things for myself, I've become a healthier, happier person.

Chapter Eighteen

You Don't Have to Be a Chameleon

Have you ever felt horrible and phony after saying or doing something that made you act and sound like the person or group you were around? Do you do this because you feel that other people have such desirable qualities? So do you, and you would see them if you only knew what color you really were. What color are you? What color do you want me to be? What do you want me to say? Do you have to be a chameleon just to get along in society?

God gave you your own color. You don't have to be a chameleon. You might find people coming closer to you and you may have more real friends once people know what color you really are.

Nugget: If something is said or done that you have a desire to refute or have an opinion on, show your colors.

How: Speak up in an open, honest, friendly and colorful way.

🔥 *Know your own colors. If you use other people's colors, you may end up making other people's mistakes.*
—"Captain Bob"

🔥 *As soon as you trust yourself, you will know how to live.*
**—Johann Wolfgang Von Goethe
(1749–1832)**

This is the end of the side drawer section of tools/skills which, if used, may encourage others to let you know what they need from you—and show you ways to receive what you need from them.

Chapter 19

The Staff Meeting (Marriage)

I was at a Fire Department staff meeting one day. J.R., the battalion chief, knew I was working on this book so as a joke he put the Love Bank as one of the items on the agenda. He was shocked at the reaction from the guys, particularly one manager. Barry said that he and his wife Joyce had just celebrated their fifth wedding anniversary the night before. They had been fighting all evening. (You know the worst year of marriage? It's usually the one you are in.) In frustration, because of the argument, Barry told us at our staff meeting, "Well, if she thinks she can cut me off, I've been there before and I'm not a beginner. I can outlast her."

I told Barry, "You know, you can do hard time or you can do easy time, the choice is really yours."

Barry said, "Yeah, well, if we have to split the sheets, that's the way it will have to be." (It seems some marriages blossom. Others just wilt and die.)

I then said, "Barry, you don't want to even know how much a divorce will cost you. Why don't you check in with John," who was sitting behind me. John was currently going through his second divorce, and he was shocked that it was going to cost him $1,500 a month for the first five years. Barry and Joyce's situation truly represents the highs and the lows of the love roller coaster. Going up, it's *I love you, love you, love you*. Then speeding down, it's *I hate you, hate you, hate you*. Some people treat this situation like this is a dress rehearsal to get ready for the real thing. This *is* the real thing!

🔥 *If you're bent on revenge, you'd better dig two graves.*

No couple should ever expect their mate to be exactly what they want them to be—but they do. We constantly judge each other by our own varying standards. Personality testing can give you great insight and be a helpful tool for understanding yourself and your partner. But it doesn't exempt you from doing the ongoing work needed for a healthy relationship. When you make a commitment to someone you get every-thing from the nursery forward in terms of their life experi-ences.

If you're someone like Barry and Joyce, and you don't get separated or divorced, eventually you're going to have to come around to patch things up—no matter how tough you are. The longer you hang out there, the more the Love Bank Account will become depleted. This is hard time. The interest you pay out when you are doing hard time is very high. Once you patch things up, and you probably will, it'll just take that much longer to replenish the Love Bank Account and stop those ridiculous late charges.

🔥 *Experience is what you get when you don't get your way.*

You would think that Barry and Joyce wouldn't make it. Well, it's now six years after that incident. They still seem to fight but swing back into being crazy about each other. They consider themselves happily married. This verifies the example of Dr. Gottman's five-to-one ratio as discussed in Chapter Five.

Relationships can get so bad for some people, they really feel they wound up with the wrong person. If only they could be with the one who got away. Well, you may have heard the story about two tears going down the river of life. One tear asked the other, "Why are you crying?" The tear said, "I had this wonderful man with all these great qualities and he got away." That tear asked the first tear, "Why are you crying?" The first tear said, "I'm the one who ended up with him."

It's kind of like a country western song, "I'm so miserable without you, it's almost like having you here."

> 🔥 *A man can lose sight of everything else when he's bent on revenge, and it ain't worth it.*
> **—Louis L'Amour (1908–1988)**

The biggest cause of divorce in this country is the **inability to change selfish behavior.** Being able to change is a key to real happiness. Some people get married and never really become a husband or a wife. If you don't have the skills (tools) or desire, happiness can't happen. Instead of acquiring the tools for the marriage to work, many people decide to end their marriage. Then they go down the road with the same tools to a new relationship and probably remarry. (For men, that's an average 18 to 24 months and for women 30 months.) But now the scenario is complicated by the problems of money, new rules, lots of relatives and carry-over grudges. No wonder 62% of second marriages fail. Love is not always better the second time around.

Problems in marriage can lead to ten times more depression than marriage without the same problems. It's the same for both men and women. There is elevated anxiety, depression, and other related illnesses.

The grass is always greener on the other side of the fence. But it is just as hard to chew and you've got to mow it, too. It's just different grass. You don't even want to ask what the percent of failure is for third, fourth and fifth marriages. There is no winning here. There are just degrees of losing.

 The greatest discovery of my generation is that a human being can alter his life by altering his attitudes of mind.
—William James (1842–1910)

And the figures aren't good for those who play house. There is up to a 50% greater chance of divorce in couples who cohabit before marriage. The practice is getting more popular. They think it's a way of working out the rough corners before marriage. Only one-third of these couples are still living together after two years of marriage. Many women feel it is the only way to get a commitment-phobic guy to marry them. It might not be on the guy's agenda though. Hopeful romantics? Don't buy anything that you can't leave if you have to split, especially a home.

Currently, 1,300 new second-marriage, "blended" (doesn't this word sound peaceful?) families are created each day in America. This will be the most common type of marriage in the country by the year 2000. A child today has a 45% chance that his parents will be divorced by the time he is 18 years old.

Many second (or third) marriages break up because of a quick remarriage. Individuals marry the same kind of person again in different clothes. They make some of the same mistakes. Another big cause of failure is largely due to the relationship between stepparents and children. We all parent differently, and there is no perfect way to raise a child, especially a stepchild. The paternal parent often becomes the referee and the new parent the enemy. Pressures can really mount if a newborn is added to the mix. It often doesn't blend. It's like trying to hold the relationship together with crazy glue.

In half of the new first marriages in the United States, one of the partners has come from a broken home. Studies suggest that those people who come from a broken home are more likely to use the option of divorce (64% higher for women and 33% for men.) Likewise, a person who has come from a home where a family member has committed suicide will be more prone to use suicide as a solution to his/her problems.

I was in a tiny bakery in Kona, on the big island of Hawaii. Behind me in the cooler cabinet was a cake with a sign on it that said, "Emergency Wedding Cake." I asked the gal if this was a joke. She said, "No, we get people in here on a regular basis who need a wedding cake—in as fast as an hour's time." Can't you see it, a couple of divorced folks in paradise. All their troubles are gone. So they say to each other, "Why don't we get married?" People rush into second, third and fourth marriages often because they are lonely, feeling inadequate and awfully hungry for intimacy. They would rather be in almost any relationship than have to face the pain of loneliness. They frequently feel that remarrying will solve these problems. If anything, the marital bliss might only intensify the problems. And when they come home, they might find out that it's Paradise Lost. Soon there comes the time when they must get back to paying the electric, doctor and other bills and going to the P.T.A. Love isn't blind, lovers are! And if you haven't worked out the problems that caused your first or second divorce, and gotten the new tools on board, you could be headed for another emotional black eye. Those who continue this cycle may someday find they are growing old alone. People think love will keep them together. It usually doesn't. Love is not a feeling. It's a behavior. How does your behavior show love to the one you love? Let the games begin.

If you are marrying a man who has gone through a divorce, make sure you check out the settlement papers for the financial obligations to his previous family. You might be shocked that some of your income or any raises in pay could be going to his former wife. In second or greater marriages with children coming from all sides, you will want to agree to be equal and fair with all the children. It just doesn't happen by itself, either. You need to get it as straight as possible going in or you might find your spouse's kids are receiving a wonderful education at a known university while your children have to settle for a community college.

An informal survey was done on 150 second-marriage couples. They found that only two of the couples had put all their assets together during the first two years of remarriage. Is this trust? Is this damage?

Could all this be why the marrying age is higher than ever before? The last U.S. Census reported the following:

- More than one in every nine adults lived alone. Since 1970, the number of women living alone grew by 91%; for men it grew 156%.
- There are 2.9 million unmarried couple households, an 80% increase in the last decade.
- The median age for first marriage is 26.1 for men and 23.9 for women; the highest in more than 100 years.

- Even with the declining divorce rate, many Americans are divorced; it is three times the 1970 ratio.

🔥 *We have forty million reasons for failure but not a single excuse.*
    —Rudyard Kipling (1865–1936)

Possible reasons for these changes may be that it's more socially acceptable to live with someone, or that people don't need to marry for respectability, sex or a home. Also, having grown up in an era of high divorce rates where individuals saw many of their peers' marriages destroyed could make them hesitant about getting married.

Relationships and marriage can be compared to the transmission in a car. At some point in the relationship you have to shift to the next gear in your ride toward intimacy. This becomes very difficult or impossible for some people in a relationship. Not only are they unable to shift to the next gear, they actually end up slamming on the brakes. If they can't even shift to the next gear, what's going to happen when the pressures of the relationship force the transmission into passing gear? They will probably end up on the rack at the shop getting their transmission rebuilt.

If it were somehow possible to condense all the changes that occur in the first five years of a marriage into one month, how many couples would be able to hold it together through the power struggle? The only thing that is constant is change.

According to authors Sue Klavens-Simring and Steven Simring, in their book *The Compatibility Quotient*, the most important compatibility factor is the mutual ability to deal with change. You cannot go into a relationship believing you will stay the same. (This can be the biggest shock of marriage.) The shape of a marriage can change dramatically. Other things that are important are finding each other interesting even without sex, having independent interests without being jealous of each other, and a serious commitment to making the marriage work.

🔥 *Opposites do attract, but they don't always stay together.*

Absolute negatives are active alcohol or drug abuse, physical violence, and an unstable personality such as exhibiting strong mood swings. Partners with the best chance of long-term success are those who can subordinate their individual interests to the needs of the marriage. Success often comes to couples who really get to know each other (more than six months) before marriage to see how they can negotiate, handle conflict and communicate.

🔥 *There are three rings of marriage. There is the engagement ring, the wedding ring, and the s u ffe ring.*

I've heard people joke that marriage is a compromise; and if I compromise my required 90%, my marriage just might work. This is not far from the truth. The old saying that marriage is a 50/50 proposition is wrong. It's 90/10 both ways.

What we're talking about here is strong commitment to any relationship. This is especially true in second marriages where commitment must be stronger because the stresses tend to be stronger.

Nugget: An unhealthy relationship can be related to a faulty car. It's not that the car (relationship) won't run; it will. But maybe the windshield wipers, or the air conditioner and heater won't work. You might have to get out and push the car to start it. It might not be able to climb a hill or the engine misfires and the transmission slips or won't shift. If you acquire the right tools you can jump-start that unhealthy (car) relationship and go in style down Main Street.

How: Read on. Take and practice the Nuggets of Life from the chapters in this book and put them in your tool box. When the time comes for a repair, you'll have the tools to keep your relationship running.

   Marriage is the only war where you sleep with the enemy.

Chapter 20

✳ Practice the Art of Conversation

Cat and Mouse

The art of conversation is . . . listening.

We choose what we want to listen to. We can actually tune out what we don't want to hear. I remember once in a science class, we conducted a study in which we hooked up an electrode to the auditory canal sensor of a cat's ear. We then turned on an irritating noise that the cat immediately heard. Lines appeared on an oscilloscope screen. After a short time, the lines on the oscilloscope went flat, as if the cat had stopped listening; yet the noise was still there. To prove that the cat had chosen to shut out the noise, we introduced a mouse. The noise instantly appeared and the oscilloscope went wild.

We've all been the cat, shutting out what we determine is not worth listening to. If you learn nothing more before you go to the grave, learning to really listen will make your life instantly much better. The most important tool I've learned about and added to my own tool box has been to become a better listener (and affirm/confirm that I have heard the message) to almost everyone, especially my wife. And aren't "he listens to me" and "he validates (affirms) my feelings" the top areas on our women's survey lists that make them feel loved? You bet!

And this one pays big dividends from the Love Bank Account. Just to listen. Not to fix, correct, or judge. Just to be a good listener.

Conversation is more than listening. It's active listening (your blood pressure rises and your heart rate increases), concentrating on what a person has said and reflecting on what you heard. Then affirming, confirming, and validating to the other person that you are involved in the conversation.

Actually, the art of conversation has not been lost. It has just fallen victim to the television set or been substituted with trips to the video store. Men receive most of their validation from their jobs. Ironically, most women, because of the types of jobs they have, are not always validated in their work position. In fact, it probably has a negative effect on their validation. Add to this some of the types of professions that women have. They still earn only 74¢ to the $1.00 of a man's earning power (up from 64¢ ten years ago). Over a thirty-year career, this could add up to $440,000. It could make the difference in buying a home, sending children to college, or retirement plans. In some fields, however, they are earning up to 85–95% of a man's earning power.

This hasn't changed much since biblical times when a man between 20 and 60 years of age earned 50 silver shekels, and a woman earned just 30 shekels. Single parent women are usually the ones who are left with the children after a divorce.

If we continually have ourselves jammed into the TV, how can we even begin to try to have a meaningful conversation? And if we don't talk on a regular basis, how will we be able to talk when an emergency arises?

It must be a federal law that men have to be the master at

the TV remote control channel changer, even though they can be vidiots (video retarded) and are unable to set the clock on the VCR. We dial up and down the stations not staying on any one channel for more than five seconds. This drives most women nuts. My wife will be cooking in the kitchen, look up, start to get into what is currently on the TV, look away for a moment, and then she can't focus back to what she was watching because I've already changed the channel.

I was doing the bills one day while glancing at the TV. I picked up the changer (mine has Space Command Unit written on it) and in frustration realized I was trying to change the channels with my calculator.

In response to this compulsion, the cable companies are coming out with a new feature. All you have to do is switch to a designated channel, and that channel will flip through the channels for you. You need only sit there and zone.

I'm joking when I say the problem here is that women need to speak a minimum of 38,785 words a day (it's genetic) and men need to speak only 987 words per day; and by the time men get home, they only have three words left—then they turn to conversational grunting.

Many women get pent up if they are not able to process what is on their mind. The days of doing the wash down at the river with the other women, quilting and canning bees, and having the extended family living in the same home are long gone. Working in a male environment and not having the time to be around other women is no help. Many men feel that they are stuck with this job of listening.

It's no joke. If this need goes unfulfilled by a woman's partner, it will be channeled elsewhere: to women friends, activities, hours on the phone (the cleanest place in the house could be the area within reach of the telephone cord), church, family, people in need, drugs or alcohol to mask the feelings and pain, or to another man who will stop long enough to listen to what a woman needs to say. This situation can lead to a serious affair.

It might be interesting to note that refusing to talk to another person is a form of control. You have no idea how many times we have heard, "He is driving me crazy. He will not talk to me." This is unfortunate, because if a problem exists, 60% of the problem can go away just by talking about it. Another form of control is that the person talks so much (they must have been vaccinated with a phonograph needle) that no one else can get a word in. Once you do get a chance to say something, these talkaholics interrupt, jam right back and take you out. Try to listen at least 60% of the time.

Have you ever talked to someone of the opposite sex and felt as if you were talking to someone from another country? Well, you are not far off, because we are wired differently. Women are more relational and conversational. Women use conversation with each other as an adhesive for friendships. Women sit closer, face each other, and just visit.

Men, on the other hand, are more detached. Men use conversation to gather statistics and facts, to jam and take each other out, to form strategies and solutions to fix things. Once men have got the information, they tend to stop talking. No small wonder that these two different ways of conversation can cause major problems, because women will want to talk to their mates—just talk. And while women are talking, men are trying to fix things, gather statistics, control and judge—when many women just want conversation. This situation is frustrating to most women because they don't have the opportunity to complete the loop to get all their feelings and opinions expressed. Some men pretend to listen. They will even gesture, nod, and change facial expressions so that you think they are listening. They're not. They will look past you and you can see that their mind is racing off somewhere else. Women should realize this, especially in business.

Women are more polite and will usually wait their turn in a conversation or a meeting. Your turn may never come, you will not be heard, or someone else will present your ideas before you and be the brilliant one. Interrupt, interrupt, interrupt. Men do! Then, don't build up like you're talking to your girlfriend—hit your major point right out of the blocks. Talk slowly, distinctly, loudly, and boldly. It's your turn!

It's not that men can't be good listeners. They've done it! When they are dating, they can be focused; they may even be hanging on your every word. You see, the hunt is on. They are pursuing you. Just like a good hunter, he will camouflage himself to trick you into believing he is not like other men. An expert camouflage artist will really believe he is a tree. His attentive listening to you could have been one of the reasons that attracted you to him. A guy does all this wonderful stuff that women enjoy like listening, paying special attention to their needs, and mega-doses of romance. Then, what happens? He bags his prey and it stops. The hunter takes off his disguise. The hunt is over, the romance ends.

After the hunt, a man will often revert to trying to fix, judge and control a conversation when a woman just wants a good listener. He will probably go to the couch and gain an extra 20 pounds. The hunt's over. If the relationship ended, he would go on the hunt again. He would lose the weight, buy a red sports car, and switch back to that attentive guy that women are looking for. This could be the shark-in-the-tank kind of guy. He knows all the things to say and do to have women believe that a relationship is going to happen and go somewhere. It usually doesn't once a woman realizes that there is no substance here, and the guy has commitment phobia.

If a guy can only imagine that the hunt doesn't have to end. He just needs to go on some different safaris which continue to provide the excitement and adventure. He could continue the pursuit and keep bagging his prey with attention, listening and romance. Then, he would continue to score big trophies on the hunting grounds of intimacy.

Men and women even argue differently. Some men generally think they argue in a practical, logical order, ending with a solution. Because women tend to argue more with their feelings and emotions, some men feel that they are arguing with a sniper; they don't know where the next shot is coming from.

On one particular day, my son Rob was in a discussion with his wife Nancy that escalated into an argument. Out of the blue Nancy said, "When we were in Hawaii, all you did was read your book. You did the same thing in the Bahamas." Baffled, Rob said , "That was five years ago, and I asked you if it was okay. You said yes." Nancy said, "Yeah, but you should have known it was bugging me." Rob has figured out what's going on here. Once a discussion escalates towards an argument, the file drawer from the past is opened. Any file with unresolved issues or unfinished business is fair game to throw in, no matter how long ago it occurred or what the issue is. Isn't love grand?

🔥 *Love is grand. Divorce is a hundred grand.*

If you really want to talk to a man, bring him an easy problem (as long as you don't overdo it). Please don't try to start a conversation by saying, "We need to talk."

He'll say, "About what?"

You'll say, "Us."

Although this conversation is usually a warning that the Love Bank Account could be overdrawn, this does not compute to most men. Especially in the middle of the night. Men are solution-oriented. Men are fixers. By bringing men a simple problem, you can start the conversation and go from there.

In many relationships there are issues a woman needs to talk about. The man in her life refuses to listen when she tries to bring them up. Consider this. First ask if this is a good time to talk. It might not be. He might be in the decompression chamber. If not, when would be a good time? Make an appointment (although this sounds silly, it's how many guys are wired). You can start by saying, "I need to talk about this issue. I know you probably don't want to discuss this, but I need to. I would appreciate if you would give me some sign that you are in the room. A sigh, groan, raised eyebrow or whatever." Then say what you need to say until you are done.

There might be another time when you will need to come back and talk about this subject. Maybe several times until you can let it go. Don't try to convince yourself that this is not important. **It is.** Just do it. You may be surprised that you have a better reception than you think. It will become easier after you close the door to retreat.

When women sit and talk, they usually face each other and sit closer together than men do. This is the most confrontational way to talk to a guy. It's the position he would be in to conduct business or to face conflict. This is the hunter and his prey, eye-to-eye, going for the kill. A woman prefers this position so she can make eye contact to interpret her partner's expressions. Many women prefer breaking up in person instead of over the phone just for this reason. Unless a man is in the camouflaged hunter pursuit mode, a woman should not try to have a conversation with her man sitting face to face. He could start preparing for fight or flight. The best way to talk to a man is side by side while driving or going for a walk.

A restaurant will try to seat Harriet and me across from each other. I will automatically move to her side of the table so we are side by side. This is a less threatening position for me. It allows me the opportunity to hold her hand, put my arm around her, rub the back of her neck, and give caresses. This would be tough to do from the confrontational side of the table.

A perfect opportunity is available here if you would set some time aside to get out of the house and go for a walk. This provides time to allow conversation away from the TV, kids, and the phone. If you think you are going to miss something on the television, just put in a tape and record the program.

By going for a walk, it not only provides that valuable needed time for conversation, but also the hidden benefits of exercise, some weight loss (which equates to feeling better about yourself), in addition to accomplishing one of the major Love Bank deposit goals of validating and listening to each other.

You can learn from the frustrated couple who shared an incident with us. Joyce and Reed were going to a family reunion an hour's drive away. All week long Joyce was trying to grab some of her husband's time to talk over some issues. The time was never right. The morning of the trip was hectic trying to prepare the two young boys and get on the road. As they wheeled onto the freeway with the two young ones already at each other, Reed said, "All right, you have been wanting to talk all week; we have an hour's drive, let's talk." Reed couldn't understand why Joyce was not receptive and he got a poor reaction.

There are still times when my wife wants to talk to me at a point when I'm not able to stop. If that situation occurs, I'll try to set a mutual time when we can talk. If my wife feels that the information is timely or an emergency, everything else comes to a full stop, including turning off the television set. How on earth are you ever going to listen to someone else when you are switching your attention between the TV and the person you are talking to? At the least, this is insulting.

And there are times when Harriet asks me if I want to go to a certain place or do a certain thing, like go to a dinner for single parents and their children recently. Although I wasn't wild about going, I did hear loud and clear that she really wanted me to go with *her*. So, I did. And as with most of these activities, it was a special blessing. In addition to an excellent meal, we met new people and had the opportunity to be part of their families.

You can do hard time or easy time, the choice is really yours.

Nugget: Learn to be a better listener. Affirm to the person you are listening to that you understand what he or she is saying.

How: Set time aside for conversation. Go for a walk. Listen at least 60% during a conversation. Just listen. Don't feel the need to fix, rescue, or judge. Just listen. Don't be the cat; tune in, don't tune out.

Chapter 21

✳ When Are Men Going to Get IT?

The eternal question has been asked, "When are men going to get IT?" What is IT? Most women know. They don't have to even say a word to express it. All they have to do is look at each other with that disgusted smirk, a shrug or roll of their eyes.

IT could mean many things. It could be knowing and understanding what women want, need or how they want to be treated. It could mean being treated as an equal in the relationship. It could be that men have a limited understanding of a woman's world.

Many men just can't see or comprehend the purpose in IT, and don't think it matters. IT can be compared to going out for ice cream. First though, we have to go over to your mother-in-law's house. A guy will want the ice cream, but he doesn't necessarily want to go to his mother-in-law's house to get it. If many men aren't able to ever get IT, maybe they could consider doing what is done in business—negotiate. By negotiating for what they need to make the relationship work, they can narrow the gap which separates them from "getting it."

There have been some interesting discoveries on how differently men's and women's brains operate. This could help explain why men seem never to get IT, as well as the process that takes place between men and women when they try to communicate

Research has revealed the process that takes place when the same information is given to men and women. Functional Magnetic Resonance Imaging (FMRI) scans of the brain is a new imaging technology that allows a look at how men and women use their brains in different ways. This is not going to be a contest on who has the advantage of a better brain. The brains of men and women are more alike than not, but, when given the same information, there were surprises in the results. When they gave the information to men, the FMRI showed blood flowing to the left side of the brain. This is the primitive task-oriented side of the brain.

When the same information was given to women, the blood not only flowed into the left side of the brain, it also flowed into the right side of the brain. This is the area where emotions and feelings are experienced.

This research suggests what many have believed. Women appear to have the full use of both hemispheres of their brains. The bundle of nerves (the corpus callosum) that bridges the left and right sides of the brain is 23% larger in women. There are more nerves in these bundles. This could be like having the Pentium super computer chip on the intimacy information superhighway. Some guys can become road kill on the highway to intimacy when they are overwhelmed with this overload on their system. This system could allow a woman to mix emotions and feelings from the right side of her brain with the left task side and enhance the results. This can be a great advantage in a business environment.

Could this be a clue to women's intuition? This could be why women can do multiple tasks simultaneously. Many women talk on the phone and do any number of other tasks at the same time. Some women can even break into conversation during sex. This is baffling to many men. It's not that men can't pull it off, too, but they may have to go into four wheel drive. Men have to stop and get out and switch the wheel hubs first. Then they have to get out and switch back once they are over the rough part. That's why sometimes when women are cruising along in a conversation with many points and the guy will suddenly say, "Hold on now, let me catch up and think about this for a minute." He will get a look on his face that reveals the gears are actually turning.

> ♨ *Love is being defined by a woman's yardstick. It's not surprising men fall short.*
> **—Bernie Zilbergeld**

This research suggests why women can usually see relationships clearly. Most women know what it takes to be in a good relationship. They know when the necessary ingredients are missing. Women are usually the ones who break off a relationship because they see problems. And women tend to take on the burden of the success or failure of the relationship. When it doesn't succeed, women pile more of the responsibility on why it didn't work.

With the help of another new imaging technique, researchers are able to see that when women are sad, *eight times* more of the right side of the brain (where depression takes place) glows with activity. This is as opposed to men's brains and could suggest why women are at least twice as depressed as men in this society.

This view of the emotion and feeling side of the brain could answer a question I've been asked at speaking engagements. Women often ask, "Why are men seemingly able to shut off their emotions and feelings and we can't?" Women find this inconceivable, because most women can't do it. This is a good example of how our brains work differently, and we establish different expectations of one another.

So when the eternal question is asked, "When are men going to get IT?"—what seems crystal clear to a woman might not be so to her partner. Would she be more understanding if she found out her partner was one of the 480 million who understood Chinese but she only knew English? That's how it sometimes seems to be in communicating because men and women process information differently. Most men can't get there from here. They just aren't capable of seeing IT the way you do. Not only don't they know, they don't even suspect.

Can't women tell by the blank look on men's faces now and then? I had a woman tell me recently that this was the gorilla mode. She always keeps a bunch of bananas on hand. When she attempts to communicate with her husband and he starts to get that gorilla look on his face, she hands him a banana. Some guys can be married for 20 or 30 years and still not know they are in a serious relationship.

Men will say they really try to get IT, but every time they think they're getting close, the rules seem to change. When men get to that point, many feel the following rules, which are written in humor, are very real and true.

1. The female always make the rules.
2. The rules are subject to change at any time without prior notification.
3. No male can possibly know all the rules.
4. If a female suspects the male knows all the rules, she must immediately change some of them.
5. The female is never wrong.

6. If the female is wrong, it's because of a flagrant misunderstanding which was a direct result of something the male did or said wrong.
7. If Rule 6 applies, the male must apologize immediately for causing the misunderstanding.
8. The female can change her mind at any given time.
9. The male must never change his mind without express written consent from the female.
10. The female has every right to be angry or upset at any time.
11. The male must remain calm at all times, unless the female wants him to be angry or upset.
12. The female must, under no circumstances, let the male know whether or not she wants him to be angry or upset.
13. Any attempt to document these Rules will result in bodily harm.
14. If the female has PMS, all rules are null and void.

Well, now that men know the Rules, they should be able to get IT.

So, if we recognize that men process and use their brains differently, but still can't find their way to IT, are they worth keeping? Yes, women could end their relationships and find someone else, but is it going to accomplish what they are looking for?

It's not that you or your significant other shouldn't pronounce your relationship dead. Could this be more of those unrealistic expectations? Oh, you might improve the average, but it probably won't be the 100% you're looking for. We seldom get 100% of what we want in life.

Does your partner equal 60% of what you're looking for in

the relationship? This is the bearable level. What we're looking for here is to propel you beyond bearable. How about negotiating whatever you need of the remaining 40% to make the relationship work? I know, if we really loved one another, we would automatically know what to do. We would know each other's heart's desires and dreams. Well, we have already covered the ground concerning how men and women think differently. It's hard for most men to recognize and understand what women want, even when they try. No, negotiating is not romantic and it shouldn't have to be this way, but it might be the road map that heads you toward your destination of having a better quality of life. Going around the tough learning curve on this map might direct you toward the road to intimacy you are trying to find. Do you want to be right or happy?

Nugget: If your relationship has 60% of what you're looking for, negotiate whatever you need of the remaining 40% to make it work. Remember, we seldom get 100% of what we want in life.

How: Negotiate until you have an agreement. Write it down. Yes, as in business, write it down. It will prevent amnesia later.

Chapter 22

✳ Recognize and Understand Processing

We already know that the top thing on a woman's survey list that makes her feel special and loved is, "He listens to me and he accepts and validates my feelings." At the end of the day, women usually want to talk about what happened during the day. This is *processing*. It's a way many women resolve issues and events in their minds so they can let them go. We were discussing this one day at work when Pam, from a local paging company, told us, "Men can't do women talk." This is true.

Because when women start talking it's like going on a journey. There may or may not be a final destination. Most men aren't packed (prepared) for the trip.

Many women try to use women talk with men. It just doesn't work with most men. Ladies, this guy you are trying to do women talk with is not your girlfriend.

This processing is difficult for most men to comprehend. What many women don't realize when they start talking to a man is that the *guy* radar comes on and tries to gather facts and statistics. It moves in a logical direction to fix, judge, or control a situation and ends at a concluding point which resolves an issue. **Big** clue here guys. Most of the time women aren't looking for the fix or solution. Often, most women just want a good listener like a girlfriend. As Pam told us "Two plus two doesn't have to equal four when women want to talk."

It's this processing that most men don't understand. That's because most men process in a different way. Many men try to solve their problems alone. Women often find solutions or other topics to discuss by talking. Men might do some processing during the day. Most don't want to come from work and talk about problems. It just brings back emotions and frustrations. When they get home they just want to decompress like a scuba diver coming up from a deep dive. This usually consists of working on a project in the garage, sports, playing at the computer, or surfing the channels on the TV. This is often perceived by his partner as a complete waste of time. Women don't want commercial time. They want prime time. During this surfing time, there is a lot of sorting out going on. And it's done in a way that the man doesn't need the woman's help.

This is hard for most women to understand because processing for them involves one or more other people. If you try to short circuit this decompression process, it is like opening the decompression chamber on the diver. He would get the bends, killing him and any chance you had of conversation.

Ladies, your partner probably doesn't have a clue as to what's going on when you're processing. Explain to him how to recognize and understand your need for processing. Have him repeat what he heard. He still might never fully understand. If he can only accept your need to process, it could be his most rewarding time for listening. Don't assume that your partner will know when you're going into processing. Give him a gentle reminder before you take off. Your chances of keeping his attention are better if you tell him how long it's going to take. For example, "Honey, this is going to take fifteen minutes." Then stick to the fifteen minutes.

I meet with a bunch of guys at a coffee shop each morning. Some of these guys have been meeting for 15 years. It's the closest thing to a male "Joy Luck Club." One of these guys, Bob, told me, "I would pay somebody to come in and sit while my wife talks."

Is it possible for men not to go directly into the decompression tank when they get home? You both have been immersed in the depths of the work day. There is great opportunity here once a man can understand the necessary processing many women need to go through at the end of the day. Could you meet at a comfortable sub-level depth, before he surfaces, for a quick debriefing? It probably won't take long. If a man knows all he has to do is be a good listener, he can adjust to the debriefing depth and blow off the CO_2 bubbles from his mask. Then he can go into the decompression chamber. When he comes out, he might find a better reception since the air has already been cleared. It could be like "aloha time" in Hawaii! It's easier to breathe when you're doing easy time.

When my wife Harriet would come home from work and start processing the day's events, I would do the guy thing and try to resolve the issues. Obviously, it didn't work. Now that I know the ground rules, that I don't have to come up with a solution and I won't be blamed, I just listen. It took some practice, but it has paid off big time. Now, I say a lot of "uh huhs, yes, no, amazing, hum, really," and "you're probably right." I do listen, though, because I know I could be tested.

And there are those times when women need to talk about the same subject once, twice, three times or more. This drives most guys nuts. Guys will say, "I thought we were done talking about that. Why do we have to revisit it again?" Some woman will say, "Well, he didn't listen the first, second, or consecutive times." What might be going on here is that women need to talk about the same things so many times because they need to resolve things within themselves by connecting all the dots, completing the loop, in order to process and let it go. Guys, you're not going to be done until she is done. Accept it.

If this happens, go for a walk. And practice these words. "Uh huh, yes, no, hum, really, amazing," and "you're probably right." This will keep you out of the penalty box.

I made a second presentation to an association meeting. One of the guys came up and told me that after the day I last spoke, three of the guys took their wives away for a getaway. The three guys decided to see how this worked. They would try not to fix, but just be good listeners and use the appropriate words to respond. After a while the wives asked, "Hey, what's going on here?" I inquired how the trip went? They all said, "Fabulous!"

There are those times when Harriet does ask me my opinion. When this occurs, I first ask what she thinks. Then I say, "If I understand you right, you mean this or that." Harriet often replies, "No, I mean this or that." Using this process, she sometimes comes up with the answer she is looking for. If not, I will do the guy thing and offer my solutions.

There are women, though, who don't care for this processing idea. If their partner did this, they would get mad. They really want you totally involved in the conversation. They want all your feedback, comments, the fix, possible solution, the whole deal. I honor this and so should you! Don't fool around here. Step up and go for it. Ladies, if this is what you want from your guy, don't assume he knows. You must tell him in a way he understands and can repeat it back to you.

Even knowing how this processing works, I still got into trouble when my wife was processing after work one day. I made the cardinal sin of giving a solution when none was asked for. I got my head taken off. When I realized what I had done, I said, "Time out. Cut off the roller derby jam. I did the guy thing trying to come up with the cure." When I went back into my listening mode, Harriet completed her processing, and then—*viola*—she scooted away.

One day, I moved Harriet's car out of the garage to make a repair. After I was done, I moved it onto the street so it wouldn't get dirty as I worked on my van. Later, Harriet came into the house and said, "You left my car on the street unlocked with the keys in it with all my stuff.

"You always leave my car on the street with the keys in it."

"You never care about my stuff."

I apologized. She kept going. I apologized again, and then a third time. Finally, I said, "I don't always do that. I have just said I'm sorry three times. I take full responsibility for my actions. What more can I do? I'm feeling the blame in a big way." Harriet replied, "Oh, I'm just processing." I had failed to recognize some key words for processing. "You always . . . never . . . every time." If a conversation sounds too far out in orbit, it's probably processing.

Nugget: Recognize and understand the need for processing.

How: Use the evening debriefing period when you first get home. Use a gentle reminder before you take off. Listen, really listen. You could be tested.

 You're probably right.
—"Captain Bob"

Chapter 23

✶ Oh Boy, Another Book on My Pillow

We were out at dinner one night with friends, Jim and Jo, whose marriage had been rocky for some time. They asked what we were doing, and we told them the concept of this book. Jim said, "Oh, boy, another book I'm going to find on my pillow." I told Jim it wasn't going to work like that. In this book, those chapters that speak loudest to men would have an ✶ (asterisk) beside them. Men can get into the book and cut right to the chase. If they like what they read, they will read on.

Actually, many women who read books on how to improve their marriages and relationships and who attend seminars or hear a good church sermon think, *If only my partner could read or understand this information, our lives would be better.* It's like the lyrics in the old Cole Porter song, "When are the bells going to chime, when is the poem going to rhyme?" Most men hate this. When I made that statement at a speaking engagement, one of the women asked, "Well, if they don't like this, then what do they want?" A quick look at the men's survey shows the most listed areas that make men feel they are special and loved. They are: being accepted for who they are and not having to change, and being supported in whatever venture, hobby or career they are involved in. Many men feel that women marry men hoping to change them, whereas men marry women hoping they won't.

🔥 *Women buy seven out of every ten books sold.*
That's known. But it's also known that women, ever
hopeful, buy a lot of books for men.
—The Grab Bag, L.M. Boyd

The main reason that men dislike being shown how and what to change to improve their relationships is that most men don't have the tools in their tool box to know how to process this information, or realize there is even the need for the tools. The information is foreign to most guys. Most men were not shown the necessary role model in their family of origin. When, as young men, were we able to sit down with our dads to go over the problems of life and relationships? Probably never. We probably weren't in a home that was emotionally healthy enough where our dads had the tools either.

As our conversation at dinner began to center on those things that make people feel special or loved, Jim snapped at his wife, "Well, Jo, I bet you don't know those things that make me feel loved!" Jo paused, then said calmly, "You know, Jim, you're probably right. Why don't you tell me." Silence followed—Jim couldn't tell Jo because he didn't know. Jim didn't know the next day either, or the next week, or even two months later. Jim is still not in touch with his feelings enough to tell his wife what makes him feel special or loved. (See Jo's testimonial at the end of this chapter.)

You can't use the Love Bank as a weapon, as Jim tried to do. It will self-destruct.

While doing our surveys, it quickly became clear that women could say exactly what made them feel special or loved. I could say to almost any woman, "I'm writing a book. Do you know those things that make you feel loved?" The female brain (computer) does not have to go searching. In a nano second, without hesitation, most women can explain in specific terms what makes them feel loved.

Men need more time to think about it. They would say, "I'll get back to you. I'll have to think about it for awhile." But, despite this promise, I never received a survey sheet back from a man who said he would fill it out later and mail it to us; that is, unless his wife said she would fill them out later and get them to us.

I was to make a presentation at a men's retreat on a Saturday at 11:00 a.m. I met with the group the night before to explain what I was going to talk about and to pass out the survey forms. By the time I was going to speak on Saturday, most of the men still had not completed their survey forms.

Sometimes it's easier for men to write down at a later time what makes them feel special or loved instead of telling about what makes them feel loved.

You may say that you didn't know what makes the special person in your life feel loved. Well now that you know, what are you going to do with the information? And why wouldn't a person want to provide those things that makes the special person in his or her life feel special and loved? First of all, he or she might not have the tools in his or her tool box to know how to begin. This is one of the goals of this book, to add those necessary tools to your tool box and transition to the five-to-one ratio.

For some people, though, not providing those things that make another person feel loved might be a control issue that keeps a mate right on the edge of insecurity. John never gave his wife a card or a gift on her birthday, Mother's Day, Christmas, or on their anniversary, even after 20 years of marriage. He says if he started doing it now, his wife would think he was cheating on her. John says his wife knows how good she has it. He might believe that, but does his wife? His actions seem mean, stingy, selfish, and lazy.

After being bombarded with information from this book, he recently gave his wife a card for her birthday. He was overwhelmed at the reception he received from just this simple act.

> 🔥 *There is no happiness in having or in getting, but only in giving.*
> **—Henry Drummond (1851–1897)**

There are some folks who will never reveal all the cards in their hand and, thus, let others know what makes them feel special or loved, nor will they do for others what makes others feel loved.

These same people also seem to be the masters of a hidden agenda. They can't possibly reveal their hidden agenda because they are acting out the woundedness (hurts) of their past. But how can any serious relationship go forward if you don't know about the past? It requires that you reveal who you really are. Revealing your hurts and insecurities may make you vulnerable and defenseless.

Instead, start by meeting another's needs. Then you're not giving up the battle, you're becoming a better person. You go from self-centered to other-centered. The giver here usually ends up receiving more than he or she gives. We've heard the comment that if you knew all about your mate, life would be boring. Experience with the Love Bank has shown that if you work on those things that make your mate feel special and loved, his or her self-esteem will become renewed and elevated. It's like a piano that is out of tune. You become the tuning fork, using the Love Bank to fine-tune your relationship.

And, as in giving of yourself, you will also improve your own self-esteem. It is sending the message that it is important enough for you to ask and care. Many marriages and relationships have never been better since they began using the Love Bank Account. And this has not just been a momentary or temporary change. My own marriage has never been better in 33 years. In this process, my wife and I have become the best of friends. And it should come as no surprise that people with an increased feeling of self-esteem are easier to live with and be with.

> **Nugget:** If you help others with their esteem and with what makes them feel special or loved, it can't help but build and also improve *your* self-esteem.

> **How:** Don't expect that a book on your partner's pillow will be the guiding light. (That is, of course, unless it's this book.) Know what makes you feel specially loved before you start asking others the question. By being able to share with others what makes both of you feel loved, the magic begins, and the Love Bank Account can be a joint one.

🔥 *You give little when you give of your possessions. It is when you give of yourself that you truly give.*
—Kahlil Gibran (1883–1931)

Jo's Testimonial of the Yosemite Dinner with Jim and Friends

At first I felt that I should help Jim out of an embarrassing situation. Next, I felt attacked and manipulated and put down for being interested in such things. Finally, I realized I was in a place where telling the truth would be safe, expected and maybe just as important . . . my attempt to "fix" this situation would have set off an over-responsible alarm in the restaurant, I'm sure! In other words, I felt my boundaries were being stepped on by passing me the "hot potato" for being responsible for Jim's answer, when he really didn't know himself what made him feel loved.

This must be a basic example of a major withdrawal from the Love Bank. Instead of an opportunity for intimacy and learning, it felt like control, manipulation, avoidance, fear.

Chapter 24

The "R" Word
(Relationship)

We were out for a drive one day with our friend Gloria. Gloria was anticipating her second date with a guy who worked for a utility company. Gloria said, "I'd just like to know where this relationship is going." I pulled off the road and said, "Gloria, this is only your second date. Why does there have to be a relationship and why does it have to be going somewhere?"

Whatever happened to getting to know someone? Many women just have to know. Most guys don't share the same intensity. It's less complex for some guys.

Me happy, me stay.

Me not happy, me leave.

The word relationship has been overused, overworked and overdone. It seems that when the "R" word is used, it means that there has to be movement, direction and commitment. Sometimes, when the "R" word is plugged in, it keeps things from evolving.

When I said the above comments to my friend Vana, she was defensive at first, but then she said, "You're probably right." What Vana hears where she works is, "Well, I'll give the relationship a week and if it doesn't work out, I'm out of here." This smacks of looking for that instant gratification that has leaked into the mainstream. It is propagated by the content of many of today's popular television shows. Problems are created that are solved in gratifying ways in 30 or 60 minutes.

I hate the "R" word, but I have to use it because it's what most people identify with. As you can see, I have used the "R" word throughout these chapters. Let's hope the "R" word can sell books.

🔥 *If the TV talk shows are any reflection of the dating scene, we're all in trouble.*

Nugget: Be cautious as to how you use the "R" word. It could short-circuit your relationship from going in the desired direction.

How: If the spark is there, the relationship is going to happen anyway, no matter what you do or say; however, it will happen in its own time and way.

You may have heard of the story of Moses Mendelssohn, the great-grandfather of the well-known German composer. Moses was far from handsome. Along with a very short stature, Moses Mendelssohn had a grotesque hunchback. One day he visited a merchant in Hamburg who had a lovely daughter named Frumptie. Kind of an unusual name, but she was a lovely woman. Well, Moses fell hopelessly in love with her. But Frumptie was repulsed by the misshapen appearance of Moses with his hunchback. When it came time for him to leave, Moses gathered his courage and climbed the stairs to her room to make one last opportunity to speak with her. She was a vision of heavenly beauty, but caused him deep sadness by her refusal to look at him. After several attempts at conversation, Moses shyly asked, "Frumptie, do you believe marriages are made in heaven?"

"Yes," she said still looking at the floor. "And do you, Moses?"

"Yes, I do," he replied. "You see, in heaven, at the birth of each boy the Lord announces which girl he will marry. When I was born, my future bride was pointed out to me. Then the Lord added, 'But, Moses, your wife will be hunchback.' Right then and there I called out, 'Oh Lord, a hunchback woman would be a tragedy; please, Lord, give me the hump and let her be beautiful.'"

Then Frumptie looked up into his eyes and was stirred by some deep memory. She reached out and gave Mendelssohn her hand, and later became his devoted wife.

Chapter 25

Establish and Communicate Realistic Expectations

Is it possible that our expectations of each other are set too high, that they are unrealistic for the person we are with?

Author Dr. John Gray was at a hotel in Dallas giving his seminar, "Men Are from Mars Women Are from Venus." A local newspaper sent a man and a woman reporter to write separate columns on their impressions of Dr. Gray's presentation. The male reporter wrote that he had heard some of this stuff before. He wanted to sneak down the hall to the bar and watch the ballgame like the other men were doing.

It was the woman reporter's column that was more interesting. She commented, "If I understand this correctly, if you can get a man to do something right, you need to give him a treat, like training a dog." What was upsetting the woman reporter was that recognizing and doing what needs to be done should be as spontaneous for men as it is for women. In presenting this comment to several men about getting a treat like training a dog, their response was, "Yeah, so?" This could be IT for a lot of guys. Many men wouldn't like to be considered the trained dog. However, most men are task and conclusion oriented. Give them a clear and direct signal about what you want them to do, and they actually *might* go do it. When they are done, give them a treat. I would like to make up some t-shirts that say, **"Where's the treat? Where's the biscuit?"**

So, what's the treat that will work? What will make Pavlov's dog salivate? Ask him what treats would be effective. It could be as simple as giving recognition when a job is completed. This is foreign to most women who, themselves, are too often taken for granted for thankless jobs around the house. It's different, though, when a guy does something on his own. He usually wants some kind of recognition. If a guy wipes off the counter after making a sandwich or if, by some strange act of heaven, he cleans the toilet, he will stand there and try to get your attention. He might say, "Hey," or "Yo," pointing and tilting his head in the direction of what he just did. You might say, "Give me a break. I have better things to do." But this is your signal to give the treat of recognition that reinforces him to continue the behavior. Ruff, ruff.

I'm sure some men will resent and challenge the idea that they are like a dog in training. Most guys aren't even aware when the dog and the treat relationship occurs. Nick challenged the connection at one of my speaking engagements. That was until the host, Carol, said, "Nick, don't you remember that I called you to come over early tonight? I asked you to move the TV so we could watch the video? You brought me flowers and moved the TV. Then I gave you a drink as a treat for helping." As Nick said, "Is that what happened?" The defense rests.

There are few men or women who are able to fulfill all the desires and dreams of a partner. It's particularly difficult for men. It's not that they don't want to, it's just hard for them to get to where this takes place. Try as they might, they can only make attempts at moving in that direction. They are still uncertain, even if they get close enough to the area for visitation rights.

There is a time period in all relationships (after about one year) when both people realize that their expectations haven't been realized. It's at this time that the sometimes unrealistic expectations must die and, working together, new ones get established. If the old expectations are not allowed to die and new ones to become established, the relationship will most likely wither on its own. The couple will continue to fail to meet each other's unrealistic expectations.

To establish new, realistic and achievable expectations, a person first needs to know what he or she really wants. Many people don't know what they want. Yet they want others to know and fix whatever it is. These needs should be condensed to 15 seconds or less. Are these expectations realistic for the other person? Are they set too high? If so, one should go back to the beginning. Each person in the relationship should consider rehearsing what he or she wants with a friend. These insights can be presented to their partner. Their partner can then repeat what was heard. It might have to go back and forth a few times before it is comprehended. Each person will want the new expectation to work, so he or she should be prepared to make an adjustment after hearing the partner's input. Once agreed upon, a commitment should be secured.

Several women have said they have embraced this concept of establishing realistic expectations with favorable results. They say, "If more women could grasp this idea, they could live happier lives." They had figured out that their man was probably not suddenly going to get IT someday and fulfill all their desires and dreams. These women had lowered (changed the focus of) their expectations to a level that their man had a chance of achieving (like not always expecting a man to recognize what needs to be done). Both the man and the woman became winners at this level, especially when the man exceeded the new expectations.

Nugget: Establish and communicate new, realistic and achievable expectations.

How: Practice giving clear and direct signals about what you want. Condense it to 15 seconds or less. Ask yourself, are the expectations realistic for this person? Are they set too high? If so, go back to the beginning. Rehearse what you want with a friend. Present what you want to your partner. Then have your partner repeat what he or she heard. You might have to go back and forth a few times before it is understood. Make adjustments where needed. Write the expectations down so there is no misunderstanding later.

Chapter 26

Affection Without Sex or Sex Without Affection

Our surveys of women placed the showing of affection without leading to sex—the touching, hugging, kissing, being held, snuggling, and other actions—to be among those top things that make them feel *loved.* Just holding hands goes a long way toward satisfying this need.

We have had women express to us that they would sometimes be willing to give up the act of sex for the opportunity just to be held.

For most men, the expression of affection without having it leading to sex is foreign. This is another tool that most men don't have in their tool boxes.

Displays of affection weren't openly shown in my family, only gestures of direct sex were.

In the movie, *It's a New Life,* a story is told about a couple who had split up and was heading for a divorce. Ann Margaret told Alan Alda, "The time for sex for you was when you took off your pants, grabbed my tits, and climbed on. Sex for me started at dinner, or earlier in the afternoon when I was fertilizing the nasturtiums."

What I have come to find out with practice is that affection, touching, and caressing don't always have to lead to sex. However, when the time is appropriate for sex, especially if it is occasionally mixed with one of the above romantic gestures, sex is magnified; probably because of those deposits of affection already in the Love Bank.

Nugget: Learn to show affection without it always having to lead to Sex.

How: Give an occasional hug, touch, squeeze, holding of hands, kiss and snuggle without the thought of it leading to sex.

Chapter 27

ATM

(How to Make a Deposit in That Special Person's Love Bank)

When I'm at work, I can sometimes hear a guy talking to his wife or girlfriend on the phone. At the end of the conversation, I'll hear him say, "Me, too." This guy is dodging it. What was he responding to? Right, someone saying, "Honey, I love you." Afraid that the guys would hear him, he weaseled out with, "Me, too" or "Ditto." And how many times have you not taken the time when you are going to be late or delayed to have the courtesy to just pick up the phone (you mean there weren't any phones from where you were and the ten miles, or the hour, it took you to drive home) to let someone know your situation. Some people think this is giving up control, as if they had it. They act as if they are on a secret mission for the CIA, or in the witness protection program and they can't tell anyone where they are.

Great opportunities have been lost by not using the phone to make an electronic ATM deposit in your and that special person's Love Bank Account. A simple, "I love you, too," or a phone call saying, "I want you to know that I'm delayed and I really love you," goes a l-o-n-g w-a-y toward validating a person's feelings, and taking your relationship off hold. I don't know of any woman who has heard, "I love you," too much. I've been married over 33 years and my wife still needs the validation of hearing, "I love you." There were times when this was icky, caca. I couldn't, or I wouldn't (not now) say, "I love you."

And don't wait until you get really sick to realize that this is a special person in your life. In the hit movie, "Ghost," Molly, played by Demi Moore, didn't believe the psychic Oda Mae Brown (Whoopi Goldberg) when she said, "Sam (Patrick Swayze) said to tell you he loves you," because Molly had said, "Sam would never say that." He only said, "Ditto."

For me, not being able to say, "I love you," was another reflection of my family background. I can't ever remember my parents saying, "I love you," to each other. Saying, "I love you," was not a tool I had in my tool box. Once I got into the habit of using this new tool and finally saying, "I love you," without mumbling, it did become a lot easier. Now I don't care who hears. As a matter of fact, if I'm at work, I make sure everyone who is in earshot hears me say, "I love you, too, sweetie." Recently I heard a woman in an office talking to her husband. At the end of their conversation she said, "You love me." Not a question, but a statement. She didn't want to go through the effort of trying to drag "I love you" out of him again. She made it easy for him. All he had to do was say, "Yes," "Maybe," "Sure," or make an appropriate grunt.

I can tell my wife, "I love you," twice a day (or more) and she still wants to hear it even more. I don't know why; that's just the way it is. It's possibly gender specific. Maybe she thinks that in the last six-and-a-half hours since the last time I told her, "I love you," I've changed my mind, or I've been lying all along and now I'm going to give up the lie. I can't explain why, so I just do it, and mean it.

When I ask Harriet the "why" about this, she says it's like getting nourishment when she eats a meal. After a while she gets hungry and needs to eat again. And Harriet never misses a meal.

> **Nugget:** Say, "I love you," to your partner, even if he or she doesn't initiate, "I love you," first. Use the phone to make an electronic deposit in each other's Love Bank Account.

> **How:** Just open that slot between your nose and your chin, breathe out and say, "I love you."

Personal Experience by Dave

The concept of the electronic deposit really hit home at one of our men's retreats when Bob shared the electronic word picture with our guys. I knew it was making an impact when suddenly the guys were calling home from the retreat that very evening. With conviction, they were filling their wives' needy Love Bank Accounts with emotional deposits. It really does work!

 One's best asset is a sympathetic spouse.
—Euripides (485–406 B.C.)

Chapter 28

✳ Nesting

In the process of renting and selling property, one thing has become perfectly clear: women are the ones who generally decide on the purchasing or renting of the property. On a walk-through, most guys breeze through a house, look in the garage to see if there is a garage door opener, and then stand back by the front door waiting and ready to leave. Yes, guys can nest too; however, it's a whole different scenario for women. As soon as a woman crosses the threshold of the front door, her antenna is up and she starts the process of geometrically placing every piece of furniture she owns in the house. She also scrutinizes the color of everything—drapes, carpets, wallpaper and large appliances. And things had better be spotless or else she grabs hubby and they are gone.

What most men don't understand is that a home or an apartment, whether rented or purchased, is usually an extension of a woman's personality. This is part of nesting. It's normal. I've seen a few men try to shoehorn their wives into accepting a property they didn't like. These men are foolish. Even if they convince their wives to accept the property, they won't stay very long at that location. First, she will be depressed, then she won't have meaningful sex, and eventually the guy will do enough hard time that he will be out looking for another home. This can get to be expensive.

The clue here is not to move in anywhere until the wife

gives the husband the correct message. An incorrect message is, "I don't know," or "It really isn't clean." The correct message is, "Yes, I love this house. I could move in right now." But even this message is an incomplete statement. The complete statement is, "I could move into this house right now" (now here comes the unheard message) "with and under certain conditions." You see, there is a nesting plan here that could be as simple as moving furniture around, or the eventual complete overhaul of the entire house, including, but not limited to, the carpets, drapes, floors, wall paint, kitchen, cabinets, yards, and especially the master bedroom. "You don't expect me to sleep in that bedroom with that carpet and drapes where another man had sex with another woman, do you?"

Even if you were eventually fortunate to complete the entire house, it would be time to start all over again. And if you are looking to get into a fixer-upper and you have never done this type of work before, you might want to reconsider. By the time you do all the work and spend all the money to bring the house back up to a presentable condition, you probably could have bought one on the same block already done. Plus, you would have financed the whole package and not had to spend the time and money in the process, avoiding much family stress .

It has happened to me just like everyone else. Not long ago we finally replaced the bedroom furniture that I had brought with me when we were married. Our new furniture was not cheap, but it was on sale and we were overdue to replace my early Goodwill decor.

What I didn't know was the rest of the nesting plan. All of a sudden an interior decorator appeared with fabric, carpet samples, wallpaper, and pictures. It became perfectly clear that we couldn't put that nice furniture into the bedroom with that old carpet. And, of course, those drapes my wife had to endure for ten years couldn't possibly match the new carpet. Are you with me, friend? The decorator and my wife said they wanted my suggestions and opinions, but when I offered my ideas they looked at me as if I was the dumbest person who had ever stood up in shoes.

I had no idea how much this was costing until my wife asked me for the deposit to start the order. The amount took my breath away. You see, I was raised in a poor family and if something was still good, serviceable, and functioning, you didn't need a new one. When I was able to get a breath, I said, "No way! Where's the oxygen?" I shouldn't have said those words because I ended up eating every one of them and more as the new custom-made king size bedspread was needed to match the drapes and the footstool with the precisely match-ing fabric that we have never used were added to the list to complete the room. When the room was done, it looked as fine as the nicest places we have stayed in when we travel. It no longer had my personal "stamp" on things. But I didn't com-plain. I loved it. After all, this is part of nesting. It makes my wife feel better about our bedroom.

I get a chuckle from men moving into a new home, who say, "This is going to be *my* room." Ha! Ha! That's what you think. Trust me, there is going to be a hidden plan for that room, a plan that you are not privy to. If you're lucky, you might end up with the garage, but only if you are able to keep it clean.

One morning, months before our oldest son was to leave the nest, I was riding the stationary bike in the family room watching TV. My wife said right out of the blue, "That bike isn't going to stay there." I looked puzzled, because the bike had been there for five-and-a-half years. I said, "What are you talking about?" So, Harriet marched me up to Rob's room to show me exactly where the bike pedestal was to sit. Then she proceeded to explain what color the room would be and what carpet and furniture were going into the room.

A fellow I work with, Mike, was getting married. When his wife-to-be came over to his place, where they were going to live, she went right into the kitchen, opened up all the drawers and cabinets, and announced, "How can you function in this kitchen the way it is laid out; and how do you exist on all these white flour, sugar-coated goods?" Mike asked me what he should do. I suggested that if he ever expected to receive a decent meal, that he consider letting his bride take over the kitchen and arrange it the way she wanted it to be. It was part of nesting. It would be okay. Once they got married, they were going to get some new drapes. They had discussed the selection, but when they were there with the saleslady to place the order, instead of vertical drapes, his wife ordered a different kind. Mike said, "We had already decided." I told Mike, "You thought you had decided. *You* might have decided, but your wife really had not. It's okay, Mike, it's part of nesting."

Now add a new baby to this equation. All the rules change because you are now entering **serious nesting**. If you were the guy who was #1 or #2 occasionally, you'll drop to #5, just below the dog. You would be better off starting with a stick of dynamite in the room where the baby is going to be, because you will end up replacing anything that can be replaced, including carpet, paint, curtains, light fixtures, door handles, and much, much more. And if you make a mistake on the gender, or the wrong shade of blue you might have to do some of the work over.

And once the pride and joy arrives, you'll need to trade in that two-seater for a vehicle that a baby car-seat can be properly secured in, and one that can haul all that stuff that you need to carry just to cover the logistics of getting from one place to another. And then, **oh no**, not another baby already. Time for a new place to live. But remember to get the correct message, "I love this house, I could move in now (under certain conditions and with certain changes)."

Nugget: Nesting is probably an extension of the woman's personality. It's okay.

How: Surrender if you ever want to have any meaningful romance in your life.

Chapter 29

Accepting Life on Today's Terms

I was heading toward the phone to call my son Rob and his wife Nancy to see how they were doing. It was Tuesday morning and a television news reporter had just shown an on-site scene of the Russian River rising to flood stages. That river ran just one block from the home in Guerneville, California, where Rob, Nancy and my two-year-old grandson Trevor lived. I feared for their safety.

Before I reached the phone, it began to ring. I instinctively knew it would be Nancy.

"Dad? It's Nancy. Rob and I need help. Fast!"

"How bad is it?" I asked, my years of training as a Fire Captain taking over. "Is Rob there now?"

"Yes, but only because I was scared. He was on call Sunday at the Fire house, but I called him home," said Nancy. "We've moved all of our valuables into the highest point of the attic," she said, "and we've taken all we could from the first floor and moved it to the second. That still may not work, though. The weather bureau and Civil Defense say that we've had the worst storms in this century. The river went over the predicted thirty-four foot flood stage by Monday morning."

It was still raining—**hard**—with more to come. Rob and Nancy were without electricity, water or heat. Water from the river had risen through the front door to the second step. Because of the sixteen inches of rain that had already fallen, the forecast was that the river would rise to a record level of forty-eight feet. Nancy's due date with their second child was Thursday. It was time to get out.

When Nancy called for us to come to get them, she didn't know how they were going to get out or where they would end up. I told Nancy that I had heard on the news they were taking people out by Army Reserve helicopters. Nancy said there was absolutely no way she would get on a helicopter. They had heard that some of those already evacuated were taken to Sebastabol.

As a firefighter captain with twenty-five years service, I could have easily pushed the crisis button and experience adrenaline "code three" action. But I had been working on accepting life on terms as it is today. My wife Harriet and I prayed a simple prayer. "Lord keep our babies safe and take us to them." A feeling of calm and peace came over us.

Since we didn't know when we would catch up with our kids, we packed an overnight bag, drinks and snacks before heading out.

Many of the roads were washed out. We just kept listening to the radio notices of the roads that were still open. Surprisingly, we made good time on the normally two-and-a-half hour drive.

As we approached Sebastabol, the traffic became grid-locked. A United Postal Service truck had just pulled over from the opposite direction. The driver got out and was telling a motorist to turn left at the next intersection in order to detour around the backup.

We went about a mile down the side road and passed a firehouse. I felt they might know what was going on. We turned around and went back. Once inside, there was a fellow firefighter, Steve, who I work with in my fire department. He lives in the area and serves as a volunteer. When we told him what was going on, he said, "I just heard on the Guerneville radio channel that they were taking a pregnant woman to the bridge by Zodiac boat, then out by helicopter." (Right, Nancy, absolutely no way you would go out by helicopter).

We couldn't be sure these were our kids, but we asked where these people were being taken. We were told they were going to the Sonoma County Airport. It was getting dark. The road to the airport through Santa Rosa was still open. On the chance that it might be Nancy, we headed that way.

When we got to the airport terminal, I asked an airline person if the helicopters had brought anyone in yet. She said, "Those flights have been canceled because of darkness and lightning."

I asked, "Where have they taken those who were brought in?"

She said, "To the Veteran's Hall in town."

I asked, "Are any of those people still there?"

She said, "Maybe."

"Could they be at the airport fire station?"

"Maybe."

We drove around to the firehouse. As we got out of our van, a strange aura came over me. I sensed that something was going on here. When we ducked under the partially-opened rolled-up rear door, things went into slow motion. A big army sergeant turned around holding our two-year-old grandson Trevor. Our son looked up from an open duffel bag as Nancy walked in from another room. They looked like drowned rats. We just stood there in disbelief. The sergeant asked Trevor, "Do you know these people?" Trevor answered in a high whisper, "Yeah." They had just arrived on the last flight in a huge Army Reserve Chinook helicopter.

There was no way any of us could have planned the events that brought us together. I believe a simple prayer activated the power of the universe that provided what we, ourselves, could not do.

A few days later, I took Rob and Nancy's brother Jay back up to Guerneville so they could go in by boat and check the damage and start cleaning up. When they got to the house they were greeted with a surprise. The Great California Flood waters had stopped just below a framed prayer that was hanging on the wall in their entry way. This prayer had been a gift from Harriet's Aunt Lois and Aunt Arah Dawson from Fayetteville, North Carolina.

A week after the floods had driven them out, Rob took his family home. Two days after they settled back in, we got another call. This one was a blessing, introducing Christian Daniel Dawson Smith, seven pounds eleven ounces. Just His will.

🔥 *Coincidence is one of God's ways of remaining anonymous.*
–Doris Lessing

Nugget: Accept life on today's terms.

How: "   "   "   "   "

Chapter 30

Intuition

I don't make any major (or most minor) decisions anymore without including my wife. Even if it is just to bounce something off Harriet. I appreciate the input and the different slant she brings to the issue. Somewhere in her explanation of ideas there is some highly valued intuition. Nothing brings intuition out as clearly as the example of a financial opportunity that was available to us a couple of years ago. A partnership was being formed to build a strip shopping center and also an apartment building with retail space at street level. We knew some of the players, and this group had success in recent projects. Harriet and I discussed the project, and Harriet came right out and said , "I don't have a good feeling about this one. Let's pass." That's all I needed to hear—we were out of the offer.

Both projects failed and have caused the loss of mega-dollars for a lot of small investors. One person lost more than $100,000, with not much hope of getting it returned. Another lost his children's college education money, and because he signed on as a partner, he also could be liable for additional losses

Call it women's intuition, luck or whatever you want, but I'm a believer in it. It has only been those times that I didn't run something up the flagpole that I've gotten into risky areas.

Our friends, Fred and Leanne, bought some land a few

years ago in Southern California that really jumped in value. A developer needed Fred's land parcels to complete their proposed sub-division. Because this property was right in the center of the new proposed sub-division, Fred was in the cat-bird seat and did not know it. He didn't want to sell until the value increased more, yet he didn't want to pay the taxes on the sale. The developer kept hounding him, so finally he offered him a trade for some other parcels of land.

Fred was the president of a small corporation and, without first checking with his wife Leanne, he accepted the exchange. For good reason, Leanne was furious. She had no intentions of selling or trading. As the dust settled, they found that the new property is not in the city and is not zoned correctly. It will take a long time and a lot of money to bring the property to the development stage like the property they exchanged; and Fred wound up getting stuck with the payment of the real estate commission. All he had to do was ask Leanne what she thought of the trade. But he didn't. When the economy changed they couldn't hold out with the mortgage payments and projected costs. The property was lost to foreclosure.

According to *Daily Review* business columnist Barbara Brock, "Intuition . . . direct knowledge without evident rational thought . . . is a word rarely used in business schools or board rooms."

But that seems to be changing. A number of businesses are devoting considerable resources to teaching their employees to become more intuitive. And we're not talking about some kooky California companies. These are Fortune 500 firms. For example, Innovation Associates of Framingham, Massachusetts, has trained over 5,000 executives from companies like DEC, Proctor & Gamble, and Clorox. In the Masters of Business Administration program at Stanford University there is a long waiting list for the "Creativity In Business" course which focuses on intuition training. Why would management go to the time and expense to develop their employees' intuitive powers? The answer is simple. It pays off!

Not many of the companies that are using intuition talk about it much. They are afraid that if their clients knew what they were doing, they would lose accounts. Clearly, intuition is a touchy subject in business. Many people consider it irrational, mystical, or (horror of horrors) feminine. "No tough-minded executive would admit to using feminine intuition," says Willis Harman, author of *Higher Creativity*. But the truth is, the more people come to trust their intuition, the better it seems to work. Indeed, studies show that executives who score higher on intuition doubled their profits in a five-year period; also, top level leaders score higher on intuition than those ranking lower in the organization.

"By and large, most people use intuition," says James Mikojkovic, management consultant and Stanford University instructor. Mr. Mikojkovic spent a year studying the strategic planning processes of chief executive officers in the Silicon Valley.

It's a proven fact that the collective experience and intelligence of a group around a meeting table is higher than any one individual of the group. Couple this with intuition and the process is magnified even greater. There is one thing for sure, my wife and I are in this for the long haul; and isn't this getting back to the two most common things that women list which make them feel loved and respected: He listens to me and validates my feelings.

Nugget: Drawing on you and your spouse's intuition can be a great tool in making most minor and major decisions. Listen to yourself. Your body may give you the correct signal as to what you should do. Don't forget also to say a prayer during the decision-making process.

How: If everyone is getting on the bandwagon— beware. This should be a red flag. Gather as much information as you can to make you feel comfortable in making a decision. Wait at least one day or longer to make a decision, depending on the importance of the decision.

Chapter 31

When Do We Start Having Fun?

Are you one of those people who never relaxes? Are you the kind who never takes time to plan a trip for yourself just to have fun? Some people never acquire the tool of learning how to relax. They often make their job their hobby. They are driven people working non-stop toward an unknown goal and reward. They are so entrenched in how and why they do things, they are really surprised when others just can't do things their way. If they are not working or busy doing some organized project, they get anxious and/or depressed and all kinds of other weird feelings start surfacing.

These people are admired, revered, envied and rewarded by others because of how much they accomplish. They never miss a committee meeting or business function. What may be disguised here could be collateral damage both to the family and to the driven person. Driven individuals are loaded with impatient, unrealistic expectations of themselves and others that may never be achieved. When they fall short of their goals, they can't find a big enough club to beat themselves with. Jokingly, some people say these folks were just toilet trained too early.

These people not only have a plan, they have two or more back-up plans that they project way down the road. Seldom are the makings of these plans ever used. It's just a lot of wasted mental energy. This obsession is progressive. It doesn't get better, only worse.

 Your mind can sometimes be like a dangerous neighborhood. You shouldn't go in there alone!

These are people who could be suffering from acute seriousity (always too serious about everything). These people could be the house sergeant or stupidvisor at home, trying to micro-manage their relationship by becoming a control freak or the resident Nazi at work. They are so serious and driven, there is seldom any fun in their lives.

Author Thomas Peters delivers the point perfectly in his book, *In Search of Excellence.*

A person can become a workaholic by over committing himself financially, by making unrealistic plans, or simply by failing to recognize a personality defect. Often he may use work as an escape mechanism. Thus, he has to drive himself to the exclusion of what should be his priorities.

It is most unfortunate that we deplore drug and alcohol addicts but somehow promote and admire the work addict. We give him status and accept his estimate of himself. And all the while his family may be getting so little of his time and energy that they hardly know him.

Overwork is not the disease itself. It is a symptom of a deeper problem—of tension, of inadequacy, of a need to achieve—that may have neurotic implications. Unfortunately for the workaholic, he has no home; his house is only a branch office. He won't take a vacation, can't relax, dislikes weekends, can't wait for Monday, and continues to make his own load heavier by bringing more work onto himself. Such a person also is usually defending against having to get close to people.

Obsessive, compulsive striving for our goals is *not* the way to pursue a life of excellence.

I was a charter member of this club, working a total of 80+ hours a week on a regular job and a side business that kept growing larger no matter what I did. It was hard to take a guy like me and expect to park him on a beach where he couldn't get cranked into a project to get the needed adrenaline fix. ("What do you mean, there's no phone here?")

For me, a seven-day vacation (how come we have to go away for so long?) consisted of two-and-a-half days of decompression, one-and-a-half days of trying to enjoy, one day of quasi-depression, and two days of, "Oh Boy, we're gearing up to go home and get back to making wampum." You do know that while you're gone on vacation everyone is getting ahead of you? It's murder if you're a hammer and everything else looks like a nail.

Eventually, this drive and all the baggage that goes with it can take its toll. Around age 40, I was starting to see guys like me down the road toward age 50 who were dropping dead of heart attacks and strokes. Or their health was damaged to the point where they couldn't enjoy life and their wives (if they were still there) were stuck taking care of this mess. At that point I figured that 100% of nothing was nothing. We're not bulletproof. When do we start to slow down and enjoy the life we have left?

These people who are driven sometimes get a few clues

that it shouldn't be this way, but just as you can't park them on a beach, they can't come to a sudden stop and get off the rocket.

It has probably been a long time since these people just took a recess. Isn't it time to smell the flowers before the petals fall off?

One way to withdraw from this compulsion is to begin approaching and processing objectives differently. Start delegating more. This is difficult for a driven individual because he or she tends not to trust anyone with the delegation of *the* project. But you must attempt to delegate more and more work and the responsibility that goes along with it.

What do you think would happen if suddenly you dropped dead? You might be surprised to find out that the things you were so driven to do, and thought nobody else could tackle, were picked right up and handled by those around you whom you wouldn't delegate to. And they would probably do a better job because of the additional talent involved.

A more rational way to work would be to treat projects like Swiss cheese. Don't go at each project like a flame thrower. Slice off a task at a time, complete that task, inject some time off, and then return to slice another. Most of this book was completed a slice at a time. Eventually, you will slice the project to completion without draining your existence. I'm not saying it's easy to do. It was tough for me to do for the first three months after I decided to get off the rocket. I felt guilty when I tried to relax. I knew I had to be someplace, but I didn't know where that somewhere was. In the morning my armpits were already wet when I hadn't done anything. It was like a race engine revving up without letting the clutch out. This was truly a withdrawal symptom.

This is a good example of what it might be like to retire

suddenly when you don't have plans in place for what you are going to do. After this experience, I realized you don't retire from something, you retire to something else.

The author Harvey Mackay writes in his book, *Swim with Sharks Without Being Eaten Alive*, that if you need something done, give it to a tiger. Tigers don't have an off switch. I was the **tiger!** But I found that you can retrofit a tiger with a dimmer switch.

It's OK to slow down and acquire the tool to start enjoying your life. If you don't, someone else will enjoy it on your inheritance or your insurance money. If you don't believe this, go on a cruise. You'll see a lot of folks who waited and saved too long to start enjoying their lives. Many are now in poor health and cheated out of what they could have had. Some don't make it to the cruise at all. You might see mom using the insurance money with her sister or the ugly duckling child.

Have you tried to rationalize to yourself that this is not like you? This is magical thinking. Magical thinking is like being in the Land of Oz. You don't want to look behind the curtain. Just ask your doctor, spouse, relative or friend. These people will tell you if you qualify. And please answer these questions:

- Do you take your briefcase, laptop, pager, cell phone, or any other work when you go away?
- Do you take self-improvement reading material on vacation under the guise that it will improve your life?
- Do you check the red answer message light on the phone first thing when you return to your hotel room?

- Are you in a hurry to call home to check the phone message machine, the voice mail at work, or download your E-mail from anywhere in the universe?
- Do you work more than 47 hours per week?
- Does your employer or secretary always know how to contact you when you're on vacation?

Have you answered yes to any of these? If so, you are probably an associate member of this club.

If you want to enjoy life more, take a bigger bite. Time to get that retrofit dimmer switch.

Nugget: The following quote from Thomas Peters' book, *In Search of Excellence*, is a perfect tool for this chapter. Even if you have read this before, it bears repeating. It was written by an unknown monk as he was about to retire.

If I had my life to live over again, I'd try to make more mistakes next time. I would relax. I would limber up. I would be sillier than I have been this trip. I know of very few things I would take seriously. I would take more trips. I would climb more mountains, swim more rivers, and watch more sunsets. I would do more walking and looking. I would eat more ice cream and fewer beans. I would have more actual troubles and fewer imaginary ones.

You see, I am one of those people who live prophylactically and sensibly and sanely, hour after hour, day after day. Oh, I've had my moments, and if I had it to do over again, I'd have more of them. In fact, I'd try to have nothing else. Just moments, one after another, instead of living so many years ahead each day. I have been one of those people who never go anywhere without a thermometer, a hot water bottle, a gargle, a raincoat, aspirin, and a parachute. If I had it to do over again, I would go places, do things, and travel lighter than I have.

If I had my life to live over, I would start barefooted earlier in the spring and stay that way later in the fall. I would play more. I would ride on more merry-go-rounds. I'd pick more daisies.

 Health trumps wealth every time.
—Dr. Walter M. Bortz

Chapter 32

For the Love of a Dad

My dad was always on the run. I can't remember a time when he didn't have at least two jobs. He never slowed down.

Dad grew up in Tampa, Florida, during the Depression. He dropped out of school in the ninth grade. He shined shoes, sold papers, delivered Western Union Telegrams, fished and crabbed to help support his family. His Dad worked part-time off the hiring board on the Seaboard Railroad.

It was an unhealthy home. My dad and his two brothers were beaten by their second generation alcoholic parents. One day, dad delivered a Western Union death notice to the right address on the wrong street. He was fired. His parents told him that without that job, he couldn't live at home. Lying about his age, the next day they placed their 17-year-old son on a merchant ship.

He eventually found his way to San Francisco and married my mom. As a merchant seaman, he served in the South Pacific through World War II.

I grew up with two brothers and three sisters. My older brother is eleven months older than me. I'm a product of "you can't get pregnant while you're nursing."

With dad's drive to work and make ends meet, it was hard to get any of the love a son needed and desired. Dad seemed to never be there for me.

Papa was a multi-talented innovative man with a great

imagination. Given different circumstances, education, and direction, there is no telling where life might have taken him.

It should be no surprise that dad and mom (mom also came from an alcoholic home) became alcoholics. Unhealthiness often seems to follow unhealthiness.

There was always fighting. I was embarrassed to bring friends home. There were families who had far less financially, but were bound by nurturing love. Their kids' esteem appeared higher.

I can only remember going on a couple of family trips. They ended in disaster.

Eventually, dad bounced around to several alcoholic programs and hospitals on his downward spiral. He lived for sometime at the Salvation Army. Dad was a survivor.

Mom gave whatever love there was in the family. My dad was cheated out of the love a son needs from his father; I was, too. There was something missing in my life. It felt as if I was carrying excess baggage for a trip I could never take.

I set out to capture the love I didn't get—the cup of sugar that I needed from my dad.

Papa was on Social Security and renting a room in someone else's home. I started picking him up to go places so we could spend time together. I was trying to put the pieces of a puzzle together.

It's almost impossible to grow up in an unhealthy home without being damaged to some degree. For my own mental health, I started going to Al-Anon meetings.

This wonderful fellowship that provides tools and hope for families of alcoholics allowed me to take the focus off my dad and concentrate on living a happier life for myself.

🔥   *Pain is inevitable; misery is optional.*

On one of our outings, I was trying to explain what had been missing and the love I needed from my dad. As I looked into my father's eyes, I realized he didn't have a clue as to what I was talking about.

My father couldn't give me what he didn't have! He had never been given this tool of love from his family. This, in itself, was a great healing moment. If I got nothing else, I would be able to let the pain go. If I had waited expecting this process to start with my father, it would have probably never happened. This was a process that had to begin with myself, then with my dad and me.

I had been anxious, angry and frustrated wanting love from my dad. Now, I was careful not to overwhelm him or beat him up with my emotions for what I expected he should have known or given me. I felt it would only alienate him further.

Coming from where he had been and with his standards, dad might have thought he had done a decent job. It had taken a long time to get to this point and I wasn't going to resolve the situation quickly.

When I was a toddler, I took "baby steps" before I could walk; the same applied here with my dad. But as uncomfortable as it was at times to communicate my feelings, I tried not to place myself in the injured child or victim role. This was the only dad I had.

I continued taking dad out during the next few years. Since he never planned to go anywhere during his life, he didn't know where to go or what to do. We went on day and overnight trips. He liked to go places where he could learn something. I found myself giving my dad the love I had missed, and doing for him what he couldn't or wouldn't do for us kids when we were growing up. I still hoped and prayed I'd receive that cup of love.

Papa was staying with one of my brothers until emphysema required him to move to a care facility. I told him it was difficult for me to watch him slowly commit suicide with cigarettes. Although he stopped drinking (only because he would be kicked out of where he lived), he refused to quit smoking.

Eventually, a wheelchair provided the escape to be able to go on our trips. A good meal became a highlight.

When his condition worsened, we moved papa to a convalescent hospital near our home so two of my sisters and their families could also be a part of his life.

The call finally came. Dad was in the hospital again. This survivor was losing the battle. Emphysema was suffocating him. We circled the wagons with all the family members.

Some of us say "when we go, we want to go fast." But sometimes the Lord provides this time to provide healing for the family.

Papa had been given morphine for the pain. He was not responding to us. Then the doctor gave us a gift. He gave dad a drug called Narcan that neutralizes opiate drugs.

Within two minutes, papa woke up bright-eyed. He scanned the room, smiled, then looked right at me and said, "Thanks for everything. I didn't know how much I loved you until I got to know you." There was my cup of love.

Our family spent a joyful healing hour with papa.

When I was getting off work the next day, it struck me that it was time for me to forgive my dad for the baggage I had been carrying. He was still alive. What was I going to do, go to his gravesite or write letters to him of my forgiveness after his death? If not now, when? It needed to begin with me.

I rushed to the hospital. I told my dad that I forgave him

for all that happened when I was growing up. He acknowl-
edged that he understood. We prayed. As I left the hospital, I
had not anticipated the overwhelming relief of the burden that
I had finally released. I believe it's almost never too late.

Dad slipped away the next day, but not without giving a
son the love only a dad can give.

If you have an estranged relationship as I had and you are
waiting for the other person to take the first step, it may never
happen. You'll never know until you try. Don't expect miracles.
I found out my Dad couldn't give me what he didn't have.

Tell those around you that you love them. I know it's hard
for men to do. But get the chicken bone out of your throat and
say it. A good way to start is by ending a phone conversation
by saying, "I love you." Then, see what happens.

Chapter 33

. . . Equals I Don't Love You
(The Formula)

How come every time you want to: play golf, restore or work on a car, work late, go skiing, boating, fishing, hunting or shopping, visit with a friend, hang out with the guys, go to a game, play cards, stop by after work for a drink with the guys or gals, or any other hobby or time away from the family, **it equals I don't love you** (to your wife or husband)?

It does, doesn't it? I used to find myself in this position all the time. What I didn't understand was that I had gone to the empty well (or Love Bank Account) too many times when I hadn't made enough deposits in the Love Bank Account. Therefore, when I wanted to take off and go do something, the withdrawal on her Love Bank Account became automatically overdrawn, and I didn't have over-draft protection.

Actually, guys do know about stacking up honey do's (honey do this, honey do that) when they anticipate that they want to exercise the option of all the honey do's for a kitchen pass to get out of the house. If there is a high enough, outstanding daily balance (as you see on your bank statements) because of your consistent ongoing deposits in the Love Bank Account, don't be surprised if you start receiving the encouragement to go and do the fun things you want to do.

How do you want it? Do you want to do hard time or easy time? The choice is yours.

Nugget: If you're getting resistance when you want to do something away from the family, better check the balance on the Love Bank Account. It's probably over-drawn and you haven't established over-draft protection.

How: Keep those Love Bank deposits going into the account to keep the average daily balance high enough for the formula to work in your favor.

Personal Experience by Lorreha

Participating in outdoor athletics has always been my husband's recreational outlet. Steve would play tennis, baseball, basketball, or volleyball every day, if it were possible.

I can recall one afternoon when he was asked to meet a friend on the golf course after work and play till dark. I had also been asked to join some girlfriends that same evening for a Tupperware party. Well, when I was not able to get a sitter, I stayed home and Steve played golf.

As the evening progressed, resentment built up inside me. It wasn't that I really had to be at another Tupperware party, it was because this was Steve's third sports outing that week, and I felt it was my turn for a break.

I truly don't mind my husband's athletic desires, but I do mind when things get out of balance. Even though his intentions were not meant to make me feel neglected or less important, I did feel that way. I have come to realize that when my husband frequently expresses verbal praises of love and support, when he does things to show his thoughts are on me by helping with the dishes, bringing flowers or taking me out for a cup of coffee, it is so much easier to watch him walk out the door with his ball and glove in his hand.

Personal Experience by Jan

It's important to me, in feeling loved by my husband, to feel that I am a worthwhile and special part of his life. I look to his actions for some of this, but even more importantly I look for his enjoyment in showing it.

The actions might include anything from sitting with me in the evening or taking a walk together or planning an evening out or going away on a trip together. Any verbal or nonverbal communication from him that it was a burden, a duty or an inconvenience would totally take away my enjoyment of the experience and leave me feeling that I was not worth the time or money spent. Then, I feel unloved.

By illustration, one time we went out to dinner to celebrate our anniversary with our one-and-a-half month old premature baby in tow. When we returned to our home other business distracted my husband. He popped his head in our bedroom door just long enough to say, "That restaurant sure was expensive. We won't go there again." Then he disappeared for quite a while.

The combination of that comment and his immediate busyness upon our return home said to me, "Well, that's done. I did my duty and it sure wasn't worth the money. Now on to other things." That sure didn't make me feel very special.

Chapter 34

What Do You Want From Me?

Larry had a rough time all during his marriage. It ended in divorce. He admitted that he was not putting into the marriage those things his wife was requesting (his wife was giving him a direct signal that there was no romance in their marriage). He probably didn't have the tools in his tool box to meet his wife's needs. It was like he was going to do little or nothing in the marriage until it came to a point that she would leave. Then, he wanted to be first in refusing to let her go.

He said that when he was trying to save the marriage, in frustration he yelled at his wife, "What do you want from me?" She couldn't (or wouldn't) tell him. What probably was going on here was that she had already shut down emotionally, at least to him.

If we could have rewound the videotape of their married life to a point at which he could have established and opened a Love Bank Account, which would have provided hope for her, we would have found out what made his wife feel loved. Larry wouldn't have found himself in a position demanding "What do you want from me?" because he would have already known. Now, this fellow is out trying to establish new relationships with the same tools. He is lonely and depressed. He says he is now doing all those things that he wasn't doing while he was married just to get a date or to get a repeat date.

You can do hard time or easy time, the choice is yours.

Nugget: Find out what deposits you can make in your loved one's Love Bank Account.

How: Take a survey. Ask. Don't wait too long before you decide it's time to start making deposits. You might find out when you finally try to make a deposit that the account has been closed out.

Chapter 35

Get a Piece of Each Other's Hide

While I was working an evening shift in the fire department, we got an emergency call. When we arrived at the home and went in, we found a 53-year-old man trying to get to his feet off the kitchen floor and save his dignity. His wife, who had fled next door, had hit him on the head with a pot. The pot had a big dent in it. We asked him what had happened?

"Well," he said, "I woke up this morning just breathing, and she was already mad." We three firefighters looked at each other, then at him and said, "Buddy, we understand. We know what you mean."

It would be safe to say that his wife's Love Bank Account was overdrawn. Even under the best of times, things build up; things we say to each other get translated incorrectly along with a misunderstanding of our tone of voice. Also, our work and other outside situations of life can create stress. Then, in the blink of an eye, you and your partner are at each other. It's almost like a pressure cooker being released. Pent up anger, hostility, and all the bad feelings come to the surface. It's like we have to tear off a piece of each other's hide. It's not a pretty sight. This is the "one" in Dr. Gottman's five-to-one ratio (see Chapter 5.) This could add newness, refresh the relationship, and get things back on track.

🔥 *The Chinese word for crisis is written with two brush strokes. The first is for danger and the second for opportunity.*

One afternoon, after my wife and I had just gone over the bills (there is never any tension when you do the bills, right?), I was in the kitchen with the door closed and Harriet was in another part of the house. I noticed that Harriet had paid a bill that we had already paid the month before, which would save us $128. In excitement, I called out to Harriet loudly, because the door was closed to the kitchen, "Come in here." Harriet came rushing in. Once I showed her the dollars we were going to save, she told me not to yell at her like that because the way I yelled, she thought there had been an emergency. I tried to explain that my voice was raised because the door was closed. Believe me, I had no intention of implying any blame to her at all. I was just excited about the money I had found.

This wasn't good enough. Harriet said again not to yell at her. "Next time say, 'Harriet could you come in here please when you have a minute?'" Again I tried to explain what had happened. Emotionally, Harriet said again, "Don't do that to me again." In an instant, I was mad, so I yelled back at her. Hurt, Harriet left the room and I went right into the penalty box. After a while Harriet wanted to talk about the situation again, but as we tried to present our opinions, our emotions were still on edge. Harriet even said, "I think you have written the wrong book." I felt the trigger to the situation was an issue that probably had not been totally resolved a couple of days earlier. Harriet didn't think so.

I felt misjudged because there had been no malice in what had happened up to the point where I went off the emotional scale. Harriet was hurt because she felt I had yelled at her in frustration. We were getting nowhere. I finally said I thought we were spending too much time around each other. We had been too close. I left and went to a movie. Getting away from each other gave us time to think about what a silly thing had just happened. When I got out of the show, I called home to see if Harriet had eaten dinner yet. She had not. I said, "Why don't we go out to eat?" Okay, a date. At dinner the first thing I told Harriet was, "You need to know that I'm here for the long haul. I'm committed. I know I don't have all the tools yet, but I'm working on getting the rest." Our anger now diffused, we talked about what had happened.

Three times Harriet had asked me not to yell at her (Harriet was sending a direct signal). Harriet needed me to validate her feelings (one of the top things for women that will make them feel loved), not just yell for Harriet to come in there. She wanted me to say, "Harriet, when you get time, please, come in here." Three times I thought I was telling her what she wanted to hear.

What we worked out was that whenever a situation arose again like the one we had just gone through, before we reached the flash point each of us would have the option to call a time out. At that point the other person would stop and honor the request by simply listening to what the other person had to say. One of us would just listen until the other person was completely done. This would allow us the opportunity to stop yelling at one another and start listening.

🔥   *Are you really listening, or are you planning your rebuttal?*

According to Dr. John Gottman's study of 670 couples, about 69% of things couples argue over and over about can never be completely resolved because of the differences between us since childhood. These conflicts often lead to "gridlock." If couples could stop trying to solve these problems, and come to accept the problem and their partner at some level, they could become closer. This would lower the frustration, increasing communication, affection and acceptance.

Dr. Gottman's studies show the following about those couples who resolve conflict effectively:

- Husbands and wives are able to influence each other.

- Instead of starting an argument harshly, wives start them softly thereby preventing a full-blown argument.

- In the progress of an argument, couples are able to do the needed repair work.

- Instead of hitting gridlock, couples can dialogue about constant problems.

- Husbands are able to reduce their physiological symptoms of anger such as an increased heart rate.

Understand that in conflict your ideas of what is the truth are only yours. You can't change another just because you say so. We all make up at different times. It can be a few days before it's over.

Practice active listening. Listening is a learned skill (tool). If you don't have this skill, it can be uncomfortable and a bit frustrating when you first try to develop it. But just listening can often reveal the true feelings and emotions that need to be heard to resolve differences. Often men and women are saying the same things, however, we tend to speak different dialects. The message gets lost in the translation. Knowing this, my wife and I also agreed to ask "What do you need to hear me say?" Often we can be saying the same thing in different dialects. A new tool? You bet. It's one of the tools in the arsenal of love. It's a tool that could prevent hurt feelings, mean-ons (mad, angry, etc.), with mean words, days of silence, days of asking, "What's wrong?" and getting the angry answer, "Nothing!" Making up is so hard to do. It takes (and wastes) a lot of energy to be angry.

If you don't try to resolve the troublesome issues in your relationship, they won't simply go away. Just as the constant pressure of a weed can break through cement, unresolved issues can bring your relationship to the breaking point. Some people will say, "Let's bury the hatchet and go on with life." But these same people will always remember where they buried the hatchet. It would be unrealistic to expect to resolve every issue exactly when it occurs. It's all right to agree to disagree. And remember that not making a decision is a decision.

There are those times, though, that we need to establish an agreement on what should never be said in a relationship, especially when tempers flare. You know what they are for you. One of these put-downs will destroy twenty deposits in the love bank.

Here are a few from a national survey:

- I never liked your mother.
- I've had it with this lousy marriage.
- You don't turn me on anymore.
- I have no idea why I ever married you.

I was going over this area in a speaking presentation when a couple started giggling. They had just experienced one. George told me, "I had come out on my porch and looked down at my wife who was gardening. The bright sun was reflecting on her head. I said, 'Honey, are you losing your hair again?'" Instant overdraft from the Love Bank and into the penalty box. Sex again—maybe next February.

We always win by agreement. Build on **wins**. There are still going to be times when couples are just going to be "at" each other. It comes with the territory. It's the "one" in Dr. Gottman's five-to-one ratio. There is the good, the bad, and the ugly in all of us. However, you can't have intimacy if any of the three are missing. You can't have intimacy without conflict, but learning how to fight or disagree *fairly* and to resolve conflict is a giant leap toward intimacy.

We had a couple tell us recently that they haven't had an argument for the last 25 years. We felt sorry for them. It's almost as if the Creator slipped this one in on us (conflict). Otherwise, how else would we have the chance to be humble and be able to enjoy those great kiss-and-make-up times and the ultimate act of forgiveness?

> **Nugget:** Whenever you find yourself in a situation that is heading for the flash point, understand that this could be the "one" in Dr. Gottman's five-to-one ratio in healthy relationships. It could add newness, refresh the relationship and get it back on track. Each of you has the option to call a time out. The other person honors the request by just listening. Also, attempt to ask the question of the other person, "What do you need me to say?" You could be saying the same things in your own dialect.

> **How:** Take the needle out of the red on the emotional meter. The higher the needle goes on the emotional meter, the less rational you will become. Establish a list of what should never be said when tempers flare.

  At times a relationship is like trying to juggle chain saws while they're running.

Chapter 36

Use the Board If You Want a Man to Fix Something

When women are unsuccessful at getting their men to complete repairs and other duties, they ask them again and again. It seems that if they could just explain it to them one more time, or in a different way, the men will finally hear the message. To most men this process is viewed as "nagging."

Actually, the quickest way not to get your guy to complete repairs and help with household duties is to start blaming or nagging him. When you start blaming or nagging men they start shutting down. Most men are task oriented. If you present men with a task or problem, they usually start figuring out a solution on how to get it done or get out of doing it if they feel it is not their department.

A way to try and accomplish this goal is to put up a magic marker board where it can be seen (not on the refrigerator), and to put those items that need attention on it along with the date. If guys see the jobs to be done there on the board with a date, there is a better chance they will get the jobs done (if they are going to do them at all). If the items don't get done in a reasonable time, threaten to call in a professional to make the repairs. Worse than blaming, men don't like to pay to have an expensive professional come into their castle to make a repair without first taking a shot at it themselves.

Nugget: Don't blame or repeat to men what needs to be fixed (nagging). Men will start shutting down.

How: To get jobs done, put up a magic marker board where it can been seen. Put the task and date on the board. If the work isn't done in a reasonable period of time, threaten to call in a professional and then follow through if the work doesn't get done.

Chapter 37

Sex and Other Stuff

Sex can be the best.

Sex can be the worst.

When women are asked at our speaking engagements what they think makes men feel loved, in chorus we hear the reply, **"Sex."** Our surveys suggest this is true, but men are often reluctant to put sex down until they find out that it is OK, that it is a normal male thing and they won't be considered perverts. Then many men will say, "Yeah, that would be one for me," with thumbs up.

Since men think about sex a lot, they think women do also. Since women generally don't, they think men don't.

Since we seldom see sex listed on women's survey sheets, and sex is a strong motivating drive for most men, how do we make this work?

Women will give sex for a relationship. Men will have a relationship to get sex. Once the relationship evolves and matures with children and life in general, things will change—that's guaranteed.

If you put a dollar into a jar every time you had sex the first year of your marriage, and then took a dollar out every time you had sex after the first year, you would never empty the jar. It can be so great that first year. Sometimes you get to thinking that you have invented something that no one else has ever done. Dream on.

After the first year take all those dollars from the jar and put them in a mutual fund. By the time your first born is college age, you'll have enough money for the tuition.

Actually, an amazing 20% of the population doesn't care much about sex. The rest of us have to keep up the average. A study in Family Planning Perspectives from the University of Chicago reported that: 1) married people had sex 67 times in the past year, divorcees and never married singles 55, separated 66, widows and widowers 6; 2) frequency of sex is highest in the 30–39 age group, 78 times a year, and lowest in the 70+ group (8); 3) since marriage, 65% of women have been faithful, 30% of men; 4) an amazing 20% had been celibate during the last year. Couples with children average sex 2.2 times a week.

OK, get out the calculator. Let's see, fifty-two weeks times three—oh yes, we're way above the average, aren't we?

There are far too many people, though, who never tell their partners that they had been physically, emotionally or sexually abused. These unresolved issues will interfere with a healthy sex life. Unfortunately, there is still a stigma about having this problem and seeking help. These people live for years suffering silently and carrying the big secret. A woman shared with me that after twenty-five years of marriage, she finally told her husband she had been molested by a neighbor.

They aren't really keeping the secret at all. The truth is, the secret is keeping them. There is wonderful healing counseling for individuals and couples that could set them free.

Men seem to be more driven toward sex (we're wired this way) and sex doesn't often appear on women's surveys. Not that sex is not important to women. It's just that when you ask them what makes them feel loved, they don't automatically think of sex.

We've got to assume that sex for most women comes from their emotions and their hearts. As Billy Crystal said in the movie "City Slickers," "Women need a reason for sex, men just need a place."

It usually takes intimacy for women to want and enjoy sex. Men generally don't have these same feelings until they are involved in actually doing the sex act itself.

If your guy knew those things on your survey that made you feel loved, and he opened up a Love Bank Account, made faithful deposits to keep the average balance high enough for your withdrawals, what kind of interest and dividends would he receive in your joint account? Right . . . he would get the emotional Gold Card! His cup would runneth over.

This Is for Guys

Okay, so you have made this agreement with your partner that since you both work, you will split and share the chores and duties at home. Right? Well, although I'm not talking to all men, if you performed the same quality of work and amount of work at your regular job, you wouldn't have a job.

It's like the lyrics from an old tune, "First you say you will, and then you won't. Then you say you do, and then you don't. I'm undecided now, what am I going to do?"

So, basically, your agreement with your partner is a joke. A University of Denver study in Pittsburgh confirmed this problem. At the bottom line, consciously or subconsciously, men really don't think housework is their job. So with 74% of women 20 to 44 years of age working, and then coming home to work a second shift dealing with the children and trying to catch up on the undone chores, what kind of mood do you think the bride is going to be in at the end of the day when

Peter Cotton Tail comes along with his high beams on saying, "Is tonight the night?" Half of women prefer having sex late at night. This is usually when they can clear their minds because everything is done. But, this is the time when you can be exhausted.

Oh, if you're lucky you might get some maintenance sex, just enough to keep the edge off, but you're probably never going to receive sex the way you want it—the kind of sex you look forward to on your anniversary or birthday, the real meaningful sweet stuff, the kind to be able to leap tall buildings at a single bounce, wall-pounding, burn down, better-be-quiet-the-kids-might-hear, and aftershocks-the-next-day sex. Are you with me?

Most all men have desires for special sexual favors. Even if you were able to occasionally receive them from your partner, she may never get as emotional as you over the experience. But your chances of receiving them are greater in ways you can't imagine. The Love Bank is the magic combination.

You can't get anything like this if your spouse is at the saturation point with work, kids and family—and picking up after you. A woman told me that simply having someone watch her two-year-old and three-and-a-half-year-old boys for five minutes so she could be alone to take a shower was a relief and a great escape for her.

Women average 32.3 hours of housework a week (whether they work outside the home or not). Men average 8.7 (some do nothing; others do up to 80 hours) not including the lawn, home or auto repairs. There are men doing their fair share. They are in the minority.

For the women, it's not healthy, realistic or fair . . . it's an overwhelming "role overload."

The hurt, anger and resentment will find its way all the

way to the bedroom.

Guys, you need to know what will happen if you do more. You will find yourself living with a healthier, happier, less exhausted partner more interested in being a lover.

Because of less responsibility, couples who rent have less arguments and household chores, and more sex than those who own their own homes. Men who rent or own their own homes do about the same hours of chores. Since owning a home requires more work, who do you think is putting in the extra hours? Their partners are. It should be no surprise that there is less time for making love and more for arguments.

Your adjustment could produce more birthday and anniversary sex throughout the year. By the way, don't expect a wonderful, exciting, orgasmic experience every time you have sex with your partner. It just isn't reality. Only one out of three women receive ecstasy through sexual intercourse.

Many women will have sex with their partner when they really don't feel like it or when things aren't going right in the relationship. Afterward they feel like they have been used, like a prostitute, but they seldom utter a word of complaint.

"You mean I have to change in order to have things more to my liking? Well, I don't like that," you're likely to say. You might not. But that's the way many women are wired.

You can do hard time, or you can do easy time. The choice is really yours. Helping out by lightening the load and giving your partner love the way she wants it may get you sex the way you want it. As Keith Miller writes in *A Taste of New Wine*, "It's only love to your wife if it's love the way she wants it." A survey of your wife's Love Bank will let you know what love is for her.

A survey of how women view men:

- 42% thought men were self-centered.

- 54% of men look at women as if they are undressing them.
- 58% felt that men own them.

No Love Bank here, friends.

It should be no surprise that women are at least twice as likely as men to be depressed.

An American Psychological Association panel reported that women are often depressed because of being a female in this contemporary culture. Women at greater risk of depression are those who have suffered physical and sexual abuse (37% in the survey had suffered significant physical or sexual abuse by the age of 21); bias that persisted in forms such as lower wages than those paid to men; unhappy marriages, hormonal changes over the menstrual cycle and childbirth; and a tendency to focus on depressed feelings rather than taking steps to master them. This stigma needs to be removed. The majority of women with depression often go untreated because the depression is undetected or misdiagnosed. Women are more likely than men to be poor and to be single parents.

Since depression can easily go undiagnosed, here are a few questions from a self-rating depression scale taken from *Happiness is a Choice* by doctors Frank B. Menrith and Paul Meir:

1. I feel like crying more often now than I did a year ago.
2. I feel blue and sad.
3. I feel hopeless and helpless a good part of the time.
4. I have lost a lot of my motivation.
5. I am losing my appetite.
6. My sleep pattern has changed of late.

If you answered yes to the majority of these questions you should seek professional assistance before the depression worsens.

Often, we don't know we are depressed. At any given time, 18 million Americans suffer from depression. I was talking to my friend Paula one day and I asked her how she was doing. Her response produced red flags.

I said, "Paula, it sounds like you're depressed." She looked puzzled. She called me a few days later after some diagnoses and said, "Friend, I didn't know I was depressed. Not only am I depressed, I can identify now that I have been depressed for nine years."

🔥 *Depression is when your mind tries to beat you to death with thoughts.*
   –Rod Steiger

Are you adding to the problems or becoming part of the solution by doing those things that are necessary to prevent your lover from being depressed? You will do big hard time for this one. If you won't spend the time listening and validating feelings, learning the skills needed to carry your share of the load around the house, who will? You can't accomplish the task if you are prone on the couch. Your lady is the one who, before she leaves for work in the morning, uses 18-24 different products just to be able to walk out the door and meet the day. Men average three. She needs your emotional support for her self-esteem.

You can be a tremendous help in improving the home front by taking on some of the heavier jobs around the house. But don't start by trying to do the laundry unless your partner has signed your apprenticeship card. Go after the heavier stuff like vacuuming, and preparation and clean-up work in the kitchen. You know the difference between a cook and a chef? A chef doesn't do the dishes. Too many guys take themselves for chefs. If you can't, aren't willing or won't do a good consistent job, hire someone to come in and clean the house at least once a week. Make sure it is someone who meets your wife's standards. But, that's not letting you off the hook. You will still need to help out on a daily basis. Hire a kid to do your yard work. Take more clothes to a discount laundry. Lighten the load on your partner.

Romance, Romance

Also, don't forget romance. This is really high on the list for most women (see Chapter 48). Romance is the blood supply to good sex in your relationship. Without romance you might just get respectable sex like plugging in a toaster when your partner is like a refrigerator.

And spend some time working up to the sex act (see Chapter 26). We would be the first ones to yell at our partners not to rev up a cold engine in the car, and yet we turn around and act like a microwave for sex when women are more like crock pots. These aren't intended to be jabs at men. They're Nuggets, like a vaccination to prevent problems later.

Kissing

Out of an informal survey comes the following:

- 💜 Most women enjoy gentle kissing and holding at first.
- 💜 More passionate kissing will be welcomed as they warm up to you.

- ♥ Try to mirror your partner's kissing pattern. That's how he or she wants to be kissed.
- ♥ Guaranteed to turn most women off: hard-pressed kissing with trying to force your tongue down their throats.

A Word to Women

When women are asked what they think makes their men feel loved, once they guess the given, sex, they often guess as the men do. "Let's see, well, knowing there will be a meal prepared when he gets home. Knowing I'm taking care of his children and the home," are often answers.

In one of the lovelorn columns in a local paper, a woman wrote that she suspected a younger woman was trying to attract her man. When she asked her husband why he didn't stray, he said, "The sex at home was too great to give up." The woman was crushed that his answer was sex rather than her devotion to their home, her charm and wit. All those things do make a major difference, but if your man is not in the 20% group that doesn't have much interest in sex, sex is going to be up in the high cards like Jack, Queen, King and Ace. This is true even if he doesn't say anything about it.

In their early twenties, Donna and Judy had not yet married. During a conversation they were having, they said they thought once a man got into a relationship then he would become interested in sex. They were having trouble understanding that men are usually ready to go for it most of the time. The good Lord made men this way. Men in their thirties think about sex once every fifteen minutes. Their pupils may get up to 30% larger just viewing a picture of a nude woman.

Although men might agree to split the chores in the two-income families, in defense of their poor performance, when were they ever exposed to child care and expected to do household duties? Too many of their mothers just let them slide. So when they attempt to do a job and it doesn't get done, takes too long, or isn't completed to your satisfaction or standards, you get frustrated and end up putting hubby in the adult time-out chair and doing it yourself. It's terrible for a guy to be able to touch all the bases at work but to be tagged out at home. You think guys haven't learned this? All they have to do is play dumb and make a bigger mess to get out of doing any work.

Women can be as much of the blame as men for their helplessness. Women often go in auditioning for the part of the good wife, mother and chef, at the same time thinking to herself this guy will eventually come around and split the workload. Then, they complain afterwards for the burden they have taken on when he doesn't. It's usually the women who decide on pairing. You picked him as is, thinking your presence and love were going to be the cure for what he needed.

Once it comes time to share the load, most men don't have the skills to hit the ground running, but women shouldn't let this stop the process. Women need to stick with these men through the learning period. Pass on the heavier jobs to men.

Because women can't or won't put up with doing most of the work, things are changing. There are signs that guys are getting the message loud and clear. No work—no meaningful sex.

Dividing housework can explode a relationship. Try taking on the jobs you like. Then equally split or swap off on the rest.

Most men have good intentions when "tonight's the night. "They try to catch up on any loose ends. But, please, can't women wait until later to put on all that face cream and to do all the hair primping. Here we are in bed waiting. Oh, boy, tonight's the night. Time passes and the eyes start to close. Yawn. Oh, boy, tonight's the night. Tonight's the night . . . (snoring). Once we drop into the twilight zone, tonight usually isn't the night.

You need to understand the sex meter on guys is arousal, sex, orgasm and then sleep. If it takes too long for the first three, sleep will kick in. Sometimes guys would just as soon use the express drive-through window for sex. You're not surprised, are you? We know you like to cuddle, but you can't always count on it after sex can you?

A survey reported that 44% of the women said that their husbands wished they were more aggressive about sex. Actually only about 17% of women fit the profile of aggressive sex partners. But survey after survey found that married men were happier with their sex lives than single guys. Married men also live longer.

Ladies, when you refuse sex to your guy, he is going to take it as rejection. This is not good. Be gentle. You can tell him that your refusal is not a rejection of him. It is because of all the stresses right now. Tomorrow at 2:00 pm (a promise) would be a better time.

Sexual boredom sets in after five to seven years of marriage. Each knows what the other can and won't do. There was a national talk show on television with a panel of prostitutes. One was asked what reasons men give for coming to them. She said, "If you wives gave them what they wanted, I would be out of business." You should have heard the screaming. "No, that's not why they go to you, that's not true." What grimaces on the faces as the camera panned the audience. These women didn't want to hear this.

But we already know that sex can be a high priority for

men, and women need to know that if there is a strong enough desire and urge that either partner is not fulfilling, they'll be taking the chance of someone else out there waiting in the wings wanting to audition for the part of being Adam or Eve for the forbidden fruit. It happens all too often. Give him the kind of sex that prevents affairs. Although intercourse is more central to women's sexual satisfaction, it is only one of many sexual acts enjoyed by men. Most guys experience sexual satisfaction off a menu of variety. Using one of the many items on the menu for maintenance sex keeps the edge off until the time you are more relaxed, rested and in the mood. It probably won't take as long as it would if you argued over the situation.

Follow the advice of the thirties Fats Waller tune from the musical "Ain't Misbehavin'": "Find out what they want and give it to 'em."

A constantly heard comment from men is that after being married for awhile, those special things we used to do sexually seem to have disappeared. (Did we really do that? Yuk.) They reappear occasionally as special favors at birthday and anniversary times. It's almost as if their partner develops amnesia. She doesn't seem to remember those wonderful experiences. Please, please remember, ladies, that sex is probably really important for your guy. Cure the amnesia. Give him something to remember, often.

There is one sexual thing men request most. You know what that is. Men who enjoy and receive this sexual act from their partner on a regular basis feel better overall about their relationship. They will tell others how great their relationship is without mentioning the sex act itself.

OK, we're back together now . . .

Men and women were given quite different plumbing and areas of sensation. Unless we are not only told but shown how it works for our partner, we won't know how to operate the equipment for full performance. We will never be able to understand completely or feel the same sensations as our partner. We need show and tell sessions on what our partner needs and wants. How many times people keep silent for years because they are too embarrassed to tell the partner that moving the stimulation up one inch would bring ecstasy. We will never know unless we are taught. A good way to know is to mirror what your partner does to you. It's usually the way they want to be treated.

It is up to both men and women to be connected and keep the spark in their relationships, especially after the huge disruption when the children arrive. According to Anne Mayer, author of *How to Stay Lovers While Raising Your Children*, it's a wonder how the second child ever comes along with the cycle that's created by all the stress that ends up killing the mood and affection, which adds to more stress. You're not alone, it's that way for everybody. You must plan time together. Create romance. Take turns at giving each other a break. You both have to be keepers of the flame. Pediatrician and author Dr. Glenn M. Austin points out to parents during the prenatal interview that a parent sometimes finds, to his or her amazement, that he is jealous of all the attention focused on the new baby. Mothers normally focus their entire attention on this new gift. But none of us ever outgrow the need to be babied. And if one or the other parent feels left out they shouldn't hesitate to say, "Hey, I'm still here, too."

🔥 *Children. One is one, two is ten.*

Dr. Austin informs parents that each spouse should remember to baby the other. Mothers have a hard time; their hormones are low after a birth and they are up at night every night, feeding the baby. It's a twenty-four hour job, harder than anyone can conceive who hasn't experienced it. Luckily, the reward of having a baby makes it worthwhile. But don't forget each other in the process. Both new mothers and new fathers need help, need babying, need love.

Ever wonder why you seem to be more charged sexually when you go away? A change in the environment is a big reason. But also, if we acted at home as we do when we were away maybe things would be different. When we're away, we spend more time just being together to catch up with each other. We give attention to those areas of our lives we seem to take for granted when we're at home.

You have to get away together often to keep the flame burning. You must go without the interrupters (children). I know you feel guilty that you are not spending enough time nurturing your kids properly because you work outside the home and are tied up doing too many other things. On a recent trip we met a couple who arranged to have one child taken care of while they were away, but they couldn't bring themselves to leave *both* children at home. (They said they would take the other child the next time.) They all suffered trying to balance the trip with their three-year old. You must escape. It will be a time to recharge, to be able to spend more rested time with your offspring.

We were staying in the Marriott Hotel in Washington, D.C. Across the street was the restored turn-of-the-century Willard Hotel. A quick check found that for an extra $12.50 (which included the parking fees of $12 per day) we could move into a quasi-suite with all the great decor on a weekend special. Did we go? You bet we did. And the needle on the romance meter shot up. Go the extra distance. Pay the extra freight. It's worth it.

There is a hotel in New York that specializes in honeymoons and anniversaries. In the ballroom one evening there was a couple that had been married the day before. The band played, "I Didn't Sleep a Wink Last Night." A couple was there celebrating their third anniversary. The band played, "Night and Day." The announcer identified a couple on their 18th wedding anniversary. The band played, "Once in a While." And then a large anniversary party came in from another banquet room. As the spotlight focused on the couple that was celebrating their Fiftieth (Golden) Wedding Anniversary the husband yelled to the band leader, "Before you play 'Memories,' you better play 'We Did it Before, and We Can Do It Again.'"

Although both sexes can snore, an often-heard complaint from wives is that their husbands drive them crazy with their snoring. Working a 24-hour shift at the fire house I get first hand experience on this one. The snoring ranges from purring to, "watch out, here comes the train." Some guys talk in their sleep. We had two guys who slept next to each other. When one started talking in his sleep, the other one would sometimes answer.

My first experience with snoring came when, as a rookie, I went into the cave (dorm) to go to sleep. I thought I was just being bagged as a rookie by the snoring. But this was no drill. These were Olympic class snoring bears. The kind where you can never get in rhythm to fall asleep. There have been many times that guys have bailed out of the dorm during the night because of the snoring. Ear plugs seldom worked. You would find them dragging their mattresses into the day room or out to the engine apparatus floor.

One of our guys went to the doctor with a bruise on his leg that just wouldn't seem to heal. When the doctor suggested more tests were needed, he got concerned. That was, until the next night when he was jarred awake with a violent kick from his wife on the bruised area. She was trying to stop him from snoring again.

I came into the Fire House locker room one morning and found that a guy had gotten out of bed, walked to his locker, opened it and was leaning in, standing up sound asleep, snoring. It sounded like a pile driver. I've been known to do a little snoring myself if I'm really tired. There have been times I have felt the hard kick to my bed to roll over and stop snoring.

Our dentist has had great success with a mouth piece called the Snore Guard. It's not as cheap as sewing a golf ball on the back of the pajama top to keep you off your back, and your dental insurance won't cover it. But you could amortize the cost by the number of additional rested days that might be available for making whoopi. Harriet sent me in for the device. She says my snoring has stopped.

According to the Snore Guard people:

- One in four people snore.
- Of the 44 million who snore, most are men. (Only 20% of women snore. It's just not ladylike.)
- 20% snore at age 40. 60% snore by age 60.
- A pneumatic drill produces 71 decibels. Snoring can produce 69 decibels.
- The Snore Guard claims a 90% success rate.

Those who have used the Snore Guard claim they are less angry and it has changed their personalities. This is probably because both partners are getting the rest they need. (No, I'm not receiving a commission from Snore Guard.)

You are only adding to the cycle of being overly tired and stressed out in your relationship if you are the one who snores. We all know that the mood for sex is not going to be there when all you want to do is just make it to the bed and get some good sleep.

Nugget for men: Sex, for women, comes from their emotions and their hearts. By finding out those things that make a loved one feel loved, opening a Love Bank Account, making faithful deposits, and being a part of what needs to be done at home, you'll find your cup runneth over with what makes you feel loved.

Nugget for women: Sex is a strong motivator for most men. Men come wired this way. A man may never really fully understand your emotions and feelings. His wiring in that area is usually weak. Use the adult time-out sparingly. Cure the amnesia; find out what your partner wants and give him something he won't forget, along with the emotions and your heart, which you are so good at.

How: Talk. Both of you. Talk. Honest spoken and non-verbal discussion about your true sexual desires and those cute little names you use can create more excitement than any sex manual.

Personal Experience

Place *your* ideas, desires and fantasies in your journal and share them with your *lover.* If that doesn't light your fire, you've got wet wood.

Chapter 38

The Enemy
(Children)

I know children are a blessing from the Lord. But, how did we ever get fooled into believing these creatures running around wearing our faces were going to enrich our lives? They have colic for six months, keep you tired while they are teething, cost you like you own the money tree, cry in harmony, make you feel guilty and drive you crazy at times. They are masters at manipulation and can easily drive a wedge between Mom and Dad. They just have to have that certain meal on the menu at the restaurant. Then when it arrives at the table, they become ill after two bites. However, they have a miraculous recovery when it comes time for dessert. They often embarrass you to the bone, lie (appropriately), go through the stupid stage, stay out late without calling, possess raging hormones, and crash cars or lend their cars out so their friends can crash them. And some will experiment with drugs and alcohol. They also try to impress you with statements such as, "It's my life." They consider driving a birthright, not a privilege.

Yes, I know they are a blessing from the Lord. But having children is a big responsibility that doesn't come with a much-needed owner's manual. Kids, when they are little, will step on your toes, and when they get older they can step on your hearts. There are no requirements for having a child. It's far more difficult to get a driver's license.

Few things change a marriage the way children do. It's like stepping on a land mine when the first child arrives. Nothing could prepare you for this, because most of what happens is unpredictable. Wives become mothers, and rightly so. But far too many men aren't prepared. I feel sorry for those couples who don't have the blessing of children. They seem to travel more, have nicer clothes and cars, homes that are well kept and they are able to save a little more money. But, are they really happier? (Let's not ponder too long on that question.)

Having kids should be a rent-to-own situation, or a lease with an option to buy so that if it doesn't work out you can send them back. Some people shouldn't have pets, much less children. If you are doing any kind of a decent job as a parent, it definitely keeps you from being self-centered.

Just because you were a kid once doesn't place you in an alumni position of being an expert and knowing how to be a parent, nor does it guarantee you'll know what's going on. And, unfortunately, it's not possible to turn in your resignation if it doesn't work the way you want it to.

We all parent differently. We all have our ideas of how and what should be done to raise our offspring. Because of these differences, parenting can destroy a marriage, especially a second marriage. It's amazing that children who were conceived in love can later be used as weapons of destruction.

How many tools do we have in our tool boxes that can help us get ready to handle this experience? It is our job to civilize these young blessings, teach them how to survive in the real world, and guide them through the maze of growing up.

Parents spent 30 hours a week with their children in 1965. This has dropped to 17 hours presently. We're talking about spending time doing things together, not just communicating.

Valuable time is being missed. Families are spread all over the house because of today's technology—computer games, TV, the telephone, and the internet. We are experiencing the first generation where technology is having a huge impact on families. This is driving family members farther apart than ever before.

Reading is the foundation of learning. If a child doesn't read by the third grade there is a problem. If parents read only twenty minutes a day to their kids, the children will read one million more words each year than children who aren't read to.

How can a child do word problems if he can't read? The majority of prisoners can't read and have learning problems. Children need to be achieving instead of watching television. TV time could be spent surfing the net (no, not the games) in order to learn on a computer.

If a child doesn't do well in math or reading, his parents say he simply doesn't do well in those subjects. Parents in other countries don't assume such a situation. Look at families who immigrate here from emerging countries. They see the freedom and embrace the opportunities. They run flat-out. It's time we started doing the same thing. Hey, folks, we are in competition with other countries in this global economy. The competition for jobs is real. Only 7% of our children finish college.

According to a study conducted by Adele Esheles Gottfreid and her associates at California State University at Northridge, kids are more motivated to do well in school by their parents' encouragement. The study showed that achievement was lower when parents had rewards of toys, money, or got angry and took privileges away. "Children need to get a sense of success through the activity itself. The enhancement of mastery is its own reward."

There is less delinquency when dads are involved with their sons. Living without a father is a contributing factor in three out of four teen suicides and four in five psychiatric admissions. Seventy percent of juveniles and young adults in long-term correctional facilities did not grow up with both parents. Do you see the pattern here? Talk to your children and find out if they feel loved.

Mothers with children younger than five years old who don't have a supportive partner or group are more likely to experience clinical depression than any other group of adults.

My daughter-in-law Nancy was recovering from Lyme's Disease with two young children. Her stress level was high. Thankfully, she found M.O.P.S. (Mothers of Preschoolers). Supportive mothers' clubs are the beacon to sanity for moms. Nancy found that she was not alone in the world with her children. She found fellowship, tools, support and shared Nuggets of Life.

My son Rob and his family went to a Chinese restaurant for dinner. At the end of the meal they brought out the fortune cookies. Three-and-a-half-year-old Trevor grabbed one and ate it and tried to go for another one. His mom, Nancy, said, "Trevor, at the Chinese restaurant they bring one fortune cookie for each person." Trevor replied, "Well, I just ate yours, now I want mine."

Our grandson Trevor had just made the transfer out of pull-ups (these are the padded diaper training pants for kids) to big boy underpants. It was a cold windy day in January and my wife Harriet had taken him to the Farmer's Market. Several times she stopped to talk to friends and they commented that he must need to go to the bathroom because he kept grabbing himself. He kept saying, "No." Finally Harriet asked him, "Why are you grabbing yourself?" In great seriousness Trevor said, "I'm afraid the wind is going to blow my penis off!" One of Harriet's friends said, "Isn't that true about men. He will worry about that for the rest of his life."

Dr. James Dobson believes that the number one cause of depression in teenagers is the lack of discipline. This is not physical discipline, but rules, direction and accountability. It doesn't just happen. If you don't have or don't obtain the tools to be a capable parent and if you lack the interest to master these tools, your offspring will be sources of constant pain to you. Eighty-five percent of our personality is in place by the time we blow the candles out on the cake on our sixth birthday (not that you won't be able to change later). Children have spent more time watching TV by age six than they will ever spend the rest of their lives talking to their dads (the average is 8.5 minutes a week). We don't have to do a lot of asking ourselves as to **why we make our kids the enemy.** Don't simply give your children toys and other things, give them your time. Things can't discipline your children, only you can, with **your time**.

> The first half of our lives is ruined by our parents, and the second half by our children.
> **—Clarence Darrow**

Too many parents are softies. Kids want structure and challenge. Who's in charge? If you don't know, you could end up with your children holding you hostage. Many kids can't take "no" for an answer. "No" starts at age two . . . and it doesn't stop. Some parents don't know "no" from "know." If you can't say "no," you will end up with a highchair terrorist. Give your children structure early. Privileges aren't a birthright.

I was talking to Dorothy at the gym one morning. She is

stepmother to three teenage daughters (yes, let's go to prayer). The fourteen-year-old had requested a pager. Dorothy's reply was, "Why?"

"So I can keep in touch with my friends."

"No, I don't think so." End of story.

Saying "no" is tough for single parents and even for some married couples who end up single parents because their spouse doesn't participate in the hard task of child rearing. They struggle trying to reason with the unreasonable.

Some parents appear to have a head start on the parenting skills, whereas others just stumble around trying to figure out who these little people (their kids) are. It's not innate. It takes hard work. We think other families have it all together. If we only knew how wrong we are. And we think that if only we were more spiritual or prayed more, then our families would somehow improve.

The common problem here is that many parents refuse or don't know how to set guidelines for their children to follow. Whenever this situation exists, a void is created and we, as parents, because of what we do or don't do, may end up making our kids our enemy. You might believe that I really don't understand. Maybe so. But what I do know about damaged families from my own personal experience is that if you don't put in the necessary parenting time you can be heading for serious problems. And don't cop out by talking about "Quality Time." Come on! Try explaining what quality time is to your kids. Kids know the value of time. It's a lot more than fighting the battle of, "He's on my side of the car again. He's looking at me again. Are we there yet?" And the counter by us, "I've had enough of this. I'm turning the car around right now and we're going back home. I mean it!"

🔥   *Quality time occurs somewhere during quantity time.*

Why won't parents discipline their children? Well, some parents come from a strict upbringing and overreact by not wanting their kids to have to endure the same thing. Parents don't want to be rejected by their kids. Some can't take the pain of their children's anger. They want the siblings to love them; they don't want to be the mean guy. Many parents depend on their kids' feelings and approval for their existence. This is especially true in single parent families (who make up 25+% of all families) who use, and often need, the child for companionship and, as such, vacillate between being the buddy and the disciplinarian.

Men and women even differ on how to handle rules. With dads the rule is the rule. Moms think it's okay to reopen the rules and massage them especially with daughters.

With mothers, giving the children a bath is a nurturing experience. For dads, it can be a rushed job of "OK, that's it. Time to get out."

Some parents are victims of the "too precious child" syndrome. These parents are so overly involved with their children they feel their youngster is too fragile to discipline. This is especially true for the only child and the "it finally happened" child, whose mother's biological clock had been chiming like Big Ben.

Dr. Henry Berman, Spokane pediatrician and co-author of *The Too Precious Child*, writes that these parents can be so entangled in the specialness of their offspring that they fail to demand mature behavior from them. These parents often suffer diminished lives by allowing the sun to revolve around their children, forgetting their own needs, privacy, solitude and adult conversation.

For those parents who continue to be all things and do all things for their children through the growing years and into their 20's, the message they are really sending is that the young person is not capable of doing things for himself. This, alone, causes major problems.

So, for these parents who, for whatever reason, elect not to discipline their kids, the prognosis is not good. Pediatrician Glenn Austin, author of *Love and Power: Parent and Child*, writes that pushover parents end up with little tyrants on their hands. He presents a 35-year plus research project by the University of California at Berkeley, showing that these children don't thrive either. The study has consistently shown that children from permissive parents are immature, low in self-reliance and independence, and lack self discipline. And follow-up studies of these children-turned-teenagers show a disproportionately high number of social and academic problems.

Another long-term study conducted at UCLA revealed that although it is normal for teenagers to demonstrate some rebellion, if this disobedience of authority is not put in check it can be an indication that they have already started taking drugs or are more likely to develop a drug or alcohol problem that will continue into their mid-20's, long after their peers have grown out of it.

All parents allow their children to break the rules occasionally. According to Dr. Austin:

> Even the best parent sometimes is simply too tired or stressed out to be a consistent disciplinarian. The problem arises when parents settle into a pattern of abdicating control. These parents are reluctant to set limits, don't communicate well about what their rules

are, don't enforce rules and don't back up words with action. (They) are unable or unwilling to exert control.

Major problems also evolve when parents let the family run like a democracy, says Lee Canter, educator and co-author of *Assertive Discipline for Parents*. Mr. Canter says parents can boost their children's self-esteem by encouraging them to participate in family decisions. But he says that parents need to limit the scope of the participation or else the children will take the reins.

Mom and Dad need to be the King and Queen in this realm. We are doing our children and ourselves no favor and a great disservice to society if we send our children into life without setting out healthy discipline. By setting these goals and boundaries, you can actually bring your family closer together. It's a matter of caring for and focusing on the family. Loving your family is not a feeling, it is a behavior. And if there were a **good breeding manual** available, this would be a major chapter. Your children (and others) will only have the power you give them.

On the other end of the spectrum is the overly strict parent. Where it's "my way or the highway," parents are the resident dictators who are never off duty. A University of California at Berkeley 35+ year study also shows that harsh, punitive parenting produces troubled children.

These parents have such a death grip on their kids that it can actually cause the very problems the strict discipline was supposed to prevent. So, we are really seeking a balanced common ground with, as Dr. Austin suggests as a motto: "Firm, demanding control by warm, caring parents. Those parents who give a lot and demand a lot will have the best results."

A good way to start is to sign up for a parenting class and obtain books and information on what things are age-appropriate for your children. At different ages kids are going to be doing things that are perfectly normal for them to do at their age level. Knowing what the normal age is for a child to lie, say no, blurt out his first swear word, play doctor with your prince or princess (the royal one is always yours), get the first poor grade, act rudely, overdo makeup, experiment with drinking, or look at nude books, puts you at a little better comfort level to deal with why this is happening. The most important thing is to not overreact to a situation or try to change the normal, age-appropriate behavior, the way you experienced it from your parents.

Well, what is a normal family anyway? Who really knows? Has anyone ever seen one? The following is the best example I have seen of a "normal" home. Excerpts were taken from *Recovery* by Herbert L. Gravitz and Julie D. Bowden.

What is a "Normal" Home Like?

This question is often asked. There is no such thing as a "normal" home. Unfortunately, most of us often believe that somewhere, somehow, there exists a perfect family. This notion of the perfect family is the standard against which they judge their own family life. They have unreasonable expectations with which they compare themselves unmercifully. It appears to them that everyone else is happy and well adjusted while they are different and damaged.

1. Let us say that a "normal" family is simply one without drug or alcohol dependence, where members can talk openly about their experiences. **Healthy homes** promote children's sense of well-being; they are relatively consistent, somewhat predictable, minimally arbitrary, and only occasionally chaotic. The parents are not children

and the children are not the parents.

2. Rules are more explicit in healthy families. **Rules tend** to be realistic, humane, and not impossible to follow.

3. The rules take into account the unique feelings, beliefs, and differences of family members. It is permissible to be separate, have your own things, and your own identity. **Boundaries** between each individual are accepted, encouraged and respected. **Communications** tend to be open instead of closed.

4. **In a healthy family** children depend on adults. Children trust that they will be cared for. They are allowed to be children. In a healthy home children are taught how to cope and how to assume responsibility.

5. Children do not live in fear in a healthy family. In a healthy family children know there is someone more resourceful than themselves. **In a healthy family children know** they will not be abandoned regardless of what they do.

6. **Still, healthy families are human;** they are not perfect. That is important to know. In a healthy family there may be yelling and screaming—but not typically. There may be anxiety and tension— but not on a daily basis. There may be unhappiness—but not usually. And there may be anger and hurt—but it is not chronic.

I was so driven with self-centered compulsion I couldn't, wouldn't, didn't know how and didn't have the necessary skills and tools to know how to be a good parent. I come from a pretty crazy family. It was like feeding time at the zoo. My best skill was putting my parenting on auto-pilot, thinking it was my wife's job. Boy, was I wrong. When the walls came tumbling down (and they did) there was confusion, guilt, anxiety, depression, distrust, and blaming, and all the tragedies of deferred parenting became a monster. It was like a puzzle that had been dropped on the floor. The pieces went everywhere.

Fortunately, what I came to realize was that it wasn't too late to correct the mistakes that had been made. It was a transfusion of hope. The first thing I did was become proactive in our family. To be a part of unwinding the mess that had been created, I had to be careful not to turn my compulsion to trying to instantly fix what was broken. We decided to get counseling. This third party approach was a great investment, cutting the time and sparing emotional hurt to get the pieces of our family back together. Counseling brought fresh ideas, skills, tools and experiences where there previously were few or none.

We found that a problem child is only the identified symptom of what is wrong in the unhealthy home. We discovered that we, as the King and Queen, could set and change the rules. You really demonstrate that you love your children by setting out the rules of the realm. It's almost never too late. You must become one-minded as parents, though. If both parents don't agree on the rules to be applied, the program will fail. This can be tough if one parent has been doing the majority of the parenting in the absence of "you know who." Now, this person wants to pull rank to come in and change everything overnight. But both parents must agree. They must be one-minded, and inform the grandparents and the other relatives of the new ground rules.

Phil and Jan had an out-of-control son for whom they

tried to set new rules to re-establish sanity in the home. Jan couldn't stick to the guidelines. She was so overly responsible for young Jack that she would eventually give in to his needs and demands thinking she was helping her baby. It was too painful to watch Jack struggle with new discipline. Jan was really sabotaging any hope for a healthy family.

You also need to sit down as a family and lay out the new or revised family rules. There are many lanes of a highway you can use to accomplish the needed changes. We decided to use contracts. Four, five and six years of age is old enough to start making up contracts with children. As the children get older you can add more serious responsible contracts. Make sure all your children are present every time you set up or change a contract with each child so everyone in the family knows what is going on. No secrets. Put the contract in writing and date it.

Example: "I didn't say or agree to that."

"Well, isn't this your signature on this dated contract?"

"Oh, yeah."

This prevents amnesia. Everyone concerned should sign the contract. If the child refuses, it doesn't make any difference. The rules still apply. Everyone gets a copy of the contract and one copy goes on the refrigerator.

What do you put in the contract? Since we all parent differently it will depend on your needs and values. What is needed and acceptable for one family may not apply to another.

Be careful not to focus all the energies in your life on trying to fix your family yesterday. It took time to get where you are. It will take time to heal the family. Try to handle one thing at a time. Attempt to discuss **with**, instead of talking **to**.

In addition to clearly defined rules, there must be a loving consequence if the rule isn't followed. The rules must be clearly defined, realistic, not done to relieve **parental feelings**, and the consequence fair but enough to alter the behavior. If the consequence does not enforce the rule strongly enough, make it tougher. You don't impose the consequences. The kids do, by their actions.

Here are some examples of rules we applied in our family:

Contract Between Rob Smith and His Parents

1. The bathroom and other living areas are to be kept clean of your belongings at all times.
   Consequence: 30 minutes labor at our request.
2. The tools and the garden hose shall be put away where they belong every time you use them.
   Consequence: 30 minutes labor at our request.
3. You will be home by 11:00 p.m.

Consequence: One hour labor at our request.

The rules of this contract can be changed at any time with fair notice to meet the needs of the realm. We can discuss changing existing rules at anytime.

Maybe your home is like ours was. I couldn't get the kids to pick up after themselves. I tried everything and although I don't recommend doing the following it did work for us.

I finally decided to put everything that had not been put away between the sheets of the kids' beds. Everything. Dirty dishes, soda cans, clothes, ice trays with one ice cube, tools and even the not-rolled-up garden hose went between the sheets. The reaction was immediate. "Dad, that's not fair. Hey, I didn't leave that stuff out." It only took two days to stop the bad behavior. And it seldom happened again.

And just a side note from a firefighter. We have gone out on numerous emergency medical calls involving kids and motorcycles. It seems to be impossible for kids to drive these **murder-cycles** at a safe speed. It's like strapping a rocket between their legs. Even when they are driving correctly and 100% in the right, if a vehicle pulls out in front of them they will be the losers. The hospitals now refer to motorcycles as donor-cycles. All too often these young people end up maimed, crippled vegetables in a rest home, or as parts for a donor program.

Our kids knew that as long as they lived in our home they wouldn't own or ride on a motorcycle. No discussion. And don't give me that garbage about how economical they are.

At Christmas season one year we went out on a call where two young boys had dumped a new motorcycle while traveling 75+ miles an hour down a boulevard. The driver survived. But his seventeen-year-old friend died from a broken neck and massive internal injuries. He had just gone out for a short ride on the back of his friend's new murder-cycle.

Not while you're living in **our** home!

Setting up the rules and putting them in place was difficult at first. Consistency and persistence were the keys here. We had to be the broken record, repeating, repeating, repeating our expectations and not being sidetracked by, "Dennis gets to do it." It took a couple of weeks to get rolling. Enforcing broken rules with immediate-action consequences was essential. But once those rules were in place an amazing thing happened. The King and Queen regained control of the realm. We were careful not to blame the kids for the behavior we were responsible for in the first place. We told them we were just correcting the past mistakes. Yes, there were wrinkles and we changed the rules where and when needed, but it brought the family closer together.

No matter what happened, we looked for positive things

and were quick to praise and give encouraging feedback whenever we saw the desired changes. We were building on **wins**. It put me, as the father, at the helm to steer this family on a healthier course. We were putting back together many pieces of the puzzle of our lives.

We even set up a contract for our son Stu when he went off to college. We know many families whose kids had to drop out of college because there were no guidelines. Without the necessary guidelines you can be setting up your college student for failure.

Here are some examples of guidelines:

1. We will pay all your tuition, dorm and book costs.
2. You will receive $ x x x per month for all your incidental expenses, i.e., shampoo, haircut, gasoline, etc.
3. You will have a credit card that can only be used for emergencies. Taking your friends to dinner is not an emergency.
4. You will not take drugs.
5. You will maintain a C average or better in all classes.
6. If a special event of redeeming value comes up, we will discuss the possibility of your going.

The only consequence was that if the above rules weren't followed, the money would stop. Stuart graduated. The money never stopped.

A set of rules is a good start, but it will not guarantee that there will be no problems. Just as God has given *you* free will, He has also given it to your children. Children have to learn on their own and make their own choices and mistakes. You can give them the tools. They must do the work.

In addition to rules and guidelines, give your kids what they really need—your undivided attention. You can set up a Pal Day for each of your children. They get to pick where you go and what you do (within reason), and they have you to themselves. You could give your children tickets or coupons. Each coupon is for a specified time period of their choosing. It might seem that a kid exercises the coupon at the most inopportune time, but the reward is always there afterwards. Some companies offer adventure trips for children as young as four years old. Contact Outdoor Adventure River Specialists at 800 346-6277 or Mountain Sports at 800 444-0099.

Go to family camps and other family functions to see what healthy families do. **Make memories with your children.** I was at Lake Almanor in California watching a father and his young son when an eagle swooped down and snagged a fish from the water. The young boy yelled, "Dad, did you see that eagle catch a fish?"

"I sure did," said his dad. That child will never forget that experience. Neither will I.

🔥   *Time is the most valuable thing a man can spend.*
       −Laertus Diogenes (3rd Century)

Nothing can destroy a family faster than drugs. They are everywhere. Fifty percent of kids will take drugs. Fifty percent of parents never know. They think it's those other kids. Learn the signs and warning signals that come with drug use. Changes in behavior (not age-appropriate), a change of friends, frequent absence from school, forgetfulness, accidents, reddish eyes, loss of interest and motivation are just a few red flags.

Dr. Cherry Parker tells the story of an unhealthy family with a problem child who also was having asthma attacks. After several months of counseling, the child's asthma attacks stopped, the behavior improved and the family became healthier. At one of their last visits, the parents asked Dr. Parker when they could go back to being normal!

Nugget: Focus on your family.

How: Focus on your family. Don't lose heart. Don't quit. Hang in there just a little longer. For dramatic non-threatening family counseling advice where you can be a more competent partner, a loving parent or kid, look up this web site:

http://www.wholefamily.com

Chapter 39

Boomerang Kids

You've done your best to raise your children. You launch them out of the house. The empty nest isn't so bad. Then, they're back. Often they return because they've become accustomed to a standard that they won't be able to achieve for years, if ever. Coming of age has been extended.

The shocking part is you now have adults living in your home. The old rules don't apply. New rules are paramount because we now have a different tolerance level for dirt, expressing feelings, territorial boundaries, bringing dates home, and an estimated time of departure. They can't be coming home just to be cared for.

According to author, Jan Adams, who wrote *I'm Still Your Mother*, kids who return home need sympathy to maintain the acceptance of their independence and encouragement to develop confidence to regroup.

We have to figure out why they're back home before we can relaunch them. Then a realistic time frame is needed to accomplish this. Trying to save $12,000 first is not realistic. If they had that potential, they wouldn't be home in the first place.

This is not a democracy. The King and Queen still reign. They must also pay rent or work for rent. When our son Rob was still living at home, we started escalating his rent each month until it was going to be cheaper to get his own place.

Unknown to him, we were placing that money in a savings account and presented it to him for his deposit on his apartment. We wanted to be assured that it was a successful launch.

Often, children return with their kids because of divorce, or perhaps only the grandchildren arrive at your doorstep. This tends to be a permanent rather than a temporary situation. Many parents are resentful because they are finally getting to the time where they are enjoying their lives without children.

Having just the grandchildren arrive is becoming more common. This is truly an unplanned parenthood. Forty-six percent of these arrangements are because of drug and alcohol abuse. At best, this is just a patch job for something bigger that's broken. There are changes in lifestyle and loss of freedom by taking up to half of your home to accommodate grandchildren. Grandparents are not in touch with today's interests.

Many feel guilty about having done something wrong in raising their children. Grandparents are hesitant and can't comprehend problems created in obtaining medical benefits and enrolling kids into schools. They find themselves the oldest members of the PTA. Often times, grandparents are trying to fund this on their retirement money.

Some of their existing friends drift away because they don't have children. Their other adult children resent that their parents don't have enough time to be grandparents to their kids.

One grandparent who is raising her grandchildren sets a day aside where she is Grandma, not parent. She has special treats, activities and puts the rules away, and does the spoiling that Grandmas have a right to do.

Many grandparents feel this is enhancing their lives—that

they can do a better job now than the first time around with their kids. Or, they feel, their grandchild's life is the life they need to work on, and not their kid's life which, because of drugs or alcohol, they have no possible hope of saving.

Nugget: If a child becomes a boomerang kid, immediately set up new rules. Try to figure out why they are back. Develop a realistic plan with an estimated time for relaunching. They must pay or work for rent. Give them lots of love. If only the grandchildren are returning, get plugged into a support group through a church, AARP, and get the book by Liz Carpenter, *Unplanned Parenthood: the Confessions of a Seventy-Something Surrogate Mother.*

How: You're still the parents. The King and Queen still reign.

The following rules should apply to kids before they leave or boomerang:

> If you please . . .
> If you sleep on it, make it up.
> If you wear it, hang it up.
> If you drop it, pick it up.
> If you lay it down, put it away.
> If you eat out of it, wash it (or put it in the dishwasher).
> If you make a mess, clean it up, now.
> If you open it, close it.
> If you turn it on, turn it off.
> If you empty it, fill it up.
> If you lose it, find it yourself.
> If you borrow it, put it back where it belongs.

If you move it, return it.
If you break it, replace it.
If it rings, answer it.
If it howls or meows, feed it or let it out.
If it cries, love it.

Thank you. The Management.

Chapter 40

Eat Stress for Breakfast

Few things can throw your life out of balance like the spiraling effects of stress and fear. Because of the whiplash of downsizing and more technology, the human element in the equation has diminished.

Stress can dramatically affect our communication and relationships. How often have we heard those around us say, "I'm just overwhelmed, stressed out and unfulfilled?" We can't eliminate it. Realize, however, that you can alter the situation.

Jokingly, stress can be defined simply as the confusion created when the mind overrides the body's desire to choke the life out of someone who desperately needs it.

Some people seem to thrive on stress. For them, being under stress is just having a good day. Unfortunately, we all don't have the big "S" (Superman or Superwoman) on our chests.

According to Michael Castleman, in an article he wrote for *Prevention Magazine*, "Relationships that are under stress by the collision of work and the needs of the family don't seem to get better by themselves. Communication and planning are essential ingredients in keeping things sane, but it's difficult to achieve them when studies show that two-career couples may talk as little as fifteen minutes a day."

One of the first signs of stress with working couples is less sex. With long stressed-out days, you can get to the point of just wanting to get through with dinner, drop in front of the TV and switch your brain into neutral until it wouldn't be considered too early to put you and the kids to bed. With a loss of patience, sleeping problems, lack of a sense of humor, elevated alcohol or drug use, life can get to a point where it takes the wheels off your wagon—and life just isn't any fun anymore.

Once stress and fear step in, anxiety is not far behind. Anxiety goes hand and glove with depression. Once these unwanted friends appear, there is a downward spiraling effect that could require medical attention to stop.

Brain scan research suggests that our minds do not know the difference between imagining and the real thing. Your mind reacts the same in both situations. If you start imagining something, your body gears up as if it were really happening. F.E.A.R. (false impressions appearing real), then anxiety (the root word for anxiety means to choke or strangle) kick in and you're off and running with stress.

What should you do? Believe it or not, stress experts say, **get busy re-establishing your relationships.** By creating more quality human interactive connections you can re-balance your life. So, when the "spit hits the fan," we have a winning support team to back us up. Making small deposits of time and effort can produce instant rewards in stress reduction and elevating happiness.

A good way to start is to list those things that "stress you out." You probably didn't know what makes your partner feel special and loved, so don't be surprised when you realize that you don't know what things cause your partner to be stressed out. Just knowing and responding to the things that cause stress is an instant wire deposit to a partner's Love Bank Account. It could be simple things that never cause a spark with you, but your being five minutes late again could be devastating to your partner.

By the way, we decide who makes us angry. You don't believe that? Think about it. One person could cut into your conversation and you would welcome it. Another person could drive you berserk by doing the very same thing. We do the same thing to those we say we love. We treat people the way we see them.

🔥 *You will know when things improve, because you will think of homicide instead of suicide.*

Take the list of things that cause stress for you and divide it into two columns, one for things that you can't do anything about and one for things that you can. Being able to really see and know what items you have *no* control over can reduce your stress level and reset your priorities toward those items that you may have *more* influence over. Now prioritize the list of stresses where you can make a difference. Compare your list with your partner's. Try to combine your two lists into a family priority list. This will focus your energies on those things that most need your attention, and you'll end up with more time for the things you both want to do.

For instance, if you have an opportunity to go to an evening seminar that would fulfill a requirement for a work promotion and your partner has made plans to go out to dinner with some old friends from out of town, what do you do? Who watches the kids? A quick check of the priority list shows your job and that promotion to be above social engagements. This process can reduce the stress in making those tough decisions.

One of the major players in elevating stress is that people are overdrawing on their biological sleep bank. Sleep deprivation causes accidents, lowers productivity and makes for grouchier folks. If you change your sleep pattern by even a few hours, your mood deteriorates. Many don't know what it feels like to be wide awake, their old self, and in good humor again. In the 1800s people slept 9½ hours a day. In the 1980s it was 7½. Today, it's down to 7 hours of sleep. Our bodies aren't tricked.

The body is great at catching up on sleep debts. Having two good nights of sleep can recover moderate sleep debt. Many people sleep in or take naps on weekends.

You know when you're getting enough sleep if you don't nod off watching TV, sitting in church, driving your car, or need an alarm to wake you up, or sleep much later on your day off. A good sleep guide is to try spending an hour more in bed for a week. If you slip back to the number of hours you had been sleeping, you're probably meeting your sleeping needs.

A constant stress load wears down your immune system, according to a University of Pittsburgh Medical School study by Dr. Theresa Whiteside. Those people with the most daily aggravation and stress on the studies' "Hassles Index" have impaired immune cell activity (the body's first line of defense) and experience more illnesses of all types. People with this low killer-cell activity are more angry and confused.

But a study conducted by Dr. Jonathan Brown from the University of Washington, Seattle, shows physical fitness can protect people from most of the health problems brought on by stress. Their exposure to life's stresses had no noticeable effect on the health of those participants who had scored in the upper half on an aerobics test.

If nothing else, exercise can redirect your mind from stress and produce those wonderful endorphins in your body that make you feel better. This doesn't happen from the couch.

A good, healthy, stress-free life can also depend on good thoughts. If you are a born pessimist, constantly negative, and look at everything as black, then this situation feeds on itself and can poison you and your relationships. No one wants to be stuck living with a negative cartoon.

A study by University of Pennsylvania researcher Gregory Buchannan revealed that those people who ranked within the top 25% as being most negative in a 10-year span had the highest death rate (26 of 31 died). By contrast, only 10 of the 31 who ranked as the most optimistic had died.

The purpose here is to raise your level of tolerance to stress in order to change your "attitude," to help you have more fun, and have a better quality of life. Worry only when it's really time to worry. As Erma Bombeck said, "I have elevated worrying to an art form." (It's not time to worry yet.) You'll be less depressed and anxious.

Nugget: Recognize that stress can dramatically affect communication and relationships. Realize that you can alter the situation. Make a priority list of your "stressors." Combine them to get family priorities. Deal with those stressors where you can make the most difference. Recognize the stressors you have no control over. Get some sleep.

How: Get Busy. A little effort can produce noticeable changes in your attitude and level of enjoyment of life. Practice not being negative for five minutes. Keep doubling the time until you are a more positive optimistic person. It's a habit you can change. You might live longer with the change.

Nuggets of Life

Think freely. Smile often. Tell those you love that you love them. Rediscover old friends. Make new ones. Hope. Grow. Give. Pick some daisies. Share them. Keep a promise. Laugh heartily. Reach out. Let someone in. Hug a kid. Slow down—way down. See a sunrise. Listen to rain. Trust life. Have faith! Enjoy. Make some mistakes. Learn from them. Explore the unknown. Celebrate life! Be alive!

—Author unknown

Chapter 41

Conquer the Job Interview

🔥 *Getting the job of your dreams is like winning the lottery!*
—Jerry Price

I have been coaching job applicants for twenty-seven years. Since the job interview has a lot to do with establishing relationships and communication skills, I thought I would slip this section into the book. These Nuggets also work for promotions.

The job interview is the most misunderstood and least prepared for portion of testing. Most people don't do enough interviewing to get good at it. I've seen candidates with great credentials. Yet, they couldn't present the package at the interview. And, if you can't present the package, you don't get the job!

Our Nugget Principle has enabled applicants to improve their interview scores up to 30%. Imagine what could happen if you put into action the information in this chapter. Imagine what could happen.

The toughest thing for applicants to do is be themselves. They think they have to be someone else at the interview. Employers like to hire people they would like to work with. They are trying to find out if you mesh with what they are looking for. If you are turned down for a position, it may not be directed at you—you just might not mesh.

Everyone has a story as to how they got here. No one can tell your story. Anytime you can add a personalized experience to your answers during an interview, you will get a higher score and separate yourself from the clone candidates.

Stories are more than fact. While telling your stories, if you can re-create the emotion, the excitement, and the imagination and magic of the actual event, you draw the interviewers into the story with you. I was coaching a firefighter candidate who was telling a story of being in Yellowstone National Park the year it burned up. It wasn't a very interesting story. At one point I stopped him and asked, "Were you trapped there?" He said, "Yes, the helicopter didn't arrive and my officer took the wrong exit." Now when he tells that story the hair starts standing up on the back of your neck. You are trapped with him and you can see the hot embers dropping all around you. Do you see the difference?

You have to be the energizer bunny and keep going, and going, and going if you want to get the job of your dreams. You have to fly, drive, beg, borrow and grovel to make it happen.

The job interview is like auditioning for a play. Just as the actor prepares for an audition, you must prepare by writing a personalized script. The script is an outline about you and the important points you want to make in the interview. These points include why you want this job, what you have done to prepare for the position, why you want to work for this firm, your strengths and weaknesses, at least one strong example of why they should hire you, and any other potential interview questions of which you are aware.

Then take the script and practice, rehearse, and overlearn it with a tape recorder and video camera until it becomes second nature to you. One recorded practice session is worth ten speaking out-louds. It's a tool that will help coach you with your timing and inflection, reduce stage fright so you won't freeze up like the tin man in the Wizard of OZ show, where to cut out material, eliminate the and's, uh's, ok's, etc., and let you know if you really sound like Donald Duck. Practice makes permanent. Once it becomes second nature it will be in your subconscious where the magic takes place. This will not be canned, it will be planned.

Everyone has butterflies. The trick here is to get all the butterflies to fly in the same formation. By practicing and rehearsing, you remove up to 75% of the stage fright. You need the other 25% to carry you through.

Too many candidates get analysis paralysis by not keeping it simple at the interview (Keep It Simple, Sweetie). Just be conversational.

The job interview is fantasy land. It is not the real world. Don't try to intellectualize this process or try to bring in logic. Sometimes people who are not prepared will be pulled in to assist in your interview. My son Rob's boss was in an interview process. One candidate got the highest score she had given in three days. She gave the applicant a 95, the other raters scored 93 and 94 respectfully. As the raters were completing their scoring, the applicant said, "I'm sure glad that is over." The raters said, "Yeah", as they were completing their paper work. Then the guy said, "Because they're coming." The raters asked, "They're coming?" He said, "Yea, they're coming. The Martians are coming." The raters laughed a little and the appli-cant got mad. He had been serious. He was a genuine kook. He did so well in the interview because he lived in fantasy land. He knew the rules! Any questions?

You have 32 seconds from when you enter the room to maintain what is called the "Halo Effect." After that time you may not have a second chance. Even though there are up to six other times in an interview where you could recover, don't plan on it. In that 32 seconds the raters have already made opinions on your clothing (the strongest non-verbal statement you can make is what you wear), eye contact, body language, selection of words, and voice. According to research on communications by psychologist Albert Mehrabian, only 7% of attitudes and feelings is from our choice of words, 38% is from our voice, and 55% from our body language and facial expressions. Your body language better match what comes out of your mouth, or the raters will know it.

Deliver your presentation with a personal flair. Stanford University has done a study that demonstrates when selling a product (or yourself) only 15% of the sale has to do with your knowledge of the product; the other 85% has to deal with your *enthusiasm!* Turn it on at the interview! Practice with your tape recorder.

Don't forget that the closing part of an interview is where you call on the emotions of the interviewers to give you the job. Don't be boring by being lengthy.

Keep a vision of seeing yourself in that job. My son Rob did this when he was struggling to follow in his father's footsteps to become a firefighter. His vision was, "Seeing someone pin my badge on me" He got that job. And on that magic day, emotionally, I had the honor of pinning that badge on my son. I felt he had received a degree and career in one swoop—because he won the lottery and he didn't even buy a ticket!

Five Nuggets for a Successful Job Interview

Simple Tools to Uncomplicate The Process

1. The job interview is like auditioning for a play. You must know your lines for the part. Do you meet the minimum requirements?

2. To learn your part, make an outline of why you want this position, what you have done to prepare, why you want to work for this agency, etc. It must be about you; not a clone of someone else.

3. The outline will become your script to audition for the part. Practice, practice, rehearse, rehearse, and overlearn the part until it becomes second nature to you. This will help prevent stage fright.

4. With tremendous enthusiasm, use your new role to capture the first 32 seconds of your audition. This creates its own energy.

5. Don't reiterate in your closing. Use only the key points not already covered in your script. Without being boring, tell the interviewers that you really want the job and with your qualifications hope to be considered for the position. Make a cordial ending. Then, shut up and get out of the building.

These Nuggets are from the Power Pack Audio Cassette/Video Albums "Conquer The Job Interview." For more information call:

"Captain Bob"
5565 Black Avenue, Pleasanton, CA 94566;
Phone 888-238-3959; Fax 925-846-9650
E-Mail: captbob@verio.com
Web Page: www.eatstress.com

Chapter 42

Wampum
(Money)

Two elderly men were sitting on a park bench one day watching traffic go by. Four blocks away a Brinks armored truck was being blocked from crossing a thoroughfare because a funeral procession of cars was passing by. In frustration, the driver of the armored truck suddenly pulled into the line of cars and joined the funeral procession in order to move down the block. As the hearse and the armored truck drove by the park, one old man nudged the other and said, "Well, look at that, Ralph. You **can** take it with you!"

That sort of naiveté about money is what often leads to trouble in relationships. That's why in this chapter we're going to take a few minutes to focus on money, a.k.a. long green, wampum, cold hard cash, dough, bread, bucks, coin of the realm, etc.

It's not how much money you make, it's how much you get to keep legally. Most people are so busy trying to make money, they don't have the time to develop a plan to help them hold on to it.

In one sense, money is a parasite: it can't do anything without you. So if you're not motivated to use money wisely nothing will happen. What's your motivation for amassing your wampum? A new car? World travel? A bigger home?

Donations to your church? A comfortable retirement? There can be any number of reasons, and as long as you and your spouse are on the same wave length about money, you'll enjoy your wampum in a variety of ways.

This is not a book on money management, but ironically money is one of the biggest stressors in a relationship. It's one of the six things that didn't come with an owner's manual.

Because people come from such different paths of life, we all have our own ideas on how money should be handled. And those preconceived values will really test us and our relationship as to how we use our money. After a presentation on this topic one day, Doris shared an experience with me. She had no sooner returned from her honeymoon when her husband made a complete accounting of their finances, which included emptying out and counting the loose change in her purse. Doris said, "Talk about having second thoughts." They did work it out, though.

Money can be a focal point for a relationship. Some spouses hoard their money under the guise of saving it for a rainy day; but it never quite rains hard enough to require them to loosen that death grip on their money. This can put a great strain on a family who feels they are being robbed of the enjoyments of life. Billy Graham said, "You have never seen a hearse on the way to the cemetery towing a U-Haul trailer." You can't take it with you, no matter what our two old men were thinking.

To demonstrate how we all have different ideas on how our money is to be spent, take this little test with your partner: You are given $50,000 to spend after all your bills have been paid. How would you spend the money?

What is this money thing anyway? We have these accounts. This is my money, that's your money, and this is our money.

It's usually one person who ends up taking the reins of the money in a relationship. It doesn't matter who. It's the one who has the comfort level and the most money issues who ends up with the task.

🔥   *If you marry for money, you'll earn every penny.*

In the concentration camps during World War II, the Red Cross equally distributed blankets, food, cigarettes, and medicine to all prisoners. Like clockwork there were those people in the camps who would end up with the majority of those goods. These guys always had plenty of blankets, food and other goodies to sell or trade. Some people have a knack for bartering, negotiating, and wheeling and dealing.

🔥   *We create our own success or failure.*
—Dr. Norman Vincent Peale

Even today the wealth of this country is held by only 3% of the population. Actually, the top half of the first 1% has the really serious dough. It has been determined that if it were somehow possible to distribute this wealth equally to everyone in the United States today, within three to five years the same people would have it back. There are some who think we should divide up the wealth every Friday night.

🔥   *Destiny is not a matter of chance; it is a matter of choice. It is not a thing to be waited for; it is a thing to be achieved."*
—William Jennings Bryan
(1860–1925)

How do these people create this wealth? First of all, wealth doesn't come like a waterfall. It comes a drop at a time. There are very few legitimate get-rich-quick schemes. Successful money managers operate with goals and a plan. Most Americans lack these money-managing skills to reach these elusive goals.

If you don't have goals or a plan, how do you know where you are going?

The College for Financial Planning of Denver found the following:

1. 73% of Americans do not set financial goals.
2. 65% do not save enough.
3. 61% don't budget their incomes.

A survey by the Oppenheimer Management Corporation of New York reveals that 58% of all Americans don't know how to invest and 70% of 18- to 24-year-olds don't know the first thing about investing.

It's been said that the love of money is the root of all evil. There are others who believe it's the **lack** of money.

My friend Dan is a successful investor who often gets requests from people who want to talk about money. He first asks what their motivation is. If they don't know, they're really wasting each other's time.

Assuming they have a motivation, he then asks them how much they paid the IRS last year. Puzzled, they look at each other and one says, "Honey, how much was that check we wrote to the IRS last year? What was it, six thousand?" The other shrugs and says, "Gee, I don't remember, dear." He then chimes in with, "No, not what you wrote to the IRS when you filed your return, but what the total was you paid including your payroll deductions. It was actually more like $14,000 or more, wasn't it?"

How can people want to redirect their finances when they don't even know where they currently are financially? We know many people who invest their funds in vehicles that can't help or protect them financially. Dan then asks, "How much of this money (taxes) are you sending to Washington, D.C., for the government to hold so that it can give it back to you at a future date?" Blank looks. "Uh . . . I guess I won't get any of it back." They're right about that. Well, isn't it about time that people like this started re-investing this money in themselves instead of in the government?

About the middle of May is **tax freedom** day. This is the date on which the average U.S. taxpayer has made enough money to pay his or her taxes for the year. This date gets further into May each year because of sharp increases in state and local taxes and new federal taxes. Do you think you are going to make it in the years ahead if you don't start making your money work for you? There are ways available for you to do just **that**!

You first need to know where you are financially and then make a plan. You can start by filling out a current financial statement and budget. You can get forms from any bank or stationery store.

If you can't write out a plan, you haven't thought it through enough or don't have enough information. Being able to make a plan is the first step in reaching your financial goals.

> ♦ *The thing always happens that you really believe in; and the belief in a thing makes it happen.*
> **—Frank Lloyd Wright (1869–1959)**

Your plan should have some realistic short and long-term goals that will fit into your budget and keep you going and motivated. Don't forget to include some fun stuff in your plan. Try to put away between 5% to 10% of your after-tax income. If that is too tough, ease back a little. It's better to succeed at first than to get so frustrated you just scrap the plan.

 Perseverance is a great element of success. If you knock long enough and loud enough at the gate, you are sure to wake somebody.
—Henry Wadsworth Longfellow
(1807–1882)

Some people won't make a plan because they get destroyed if they end up short of their goals. I would rather fall one thousand dollars short of an established goal of $10,000 than to be in constant freefall with my finances. Place your plan where you can see it (on the mirror) so you can focus on the goals. Revise the plan when and as needed. When you achieve a goal put **"done"** and the date next to it so you can see your progress. Make an annual ritual of reviewing your goals and plans for a get-away trip, and set up plans and goals for the following year.

 Don't wait for your ship to come in; swim out to it.

There is an abundance of financial and money books available from book stores, many costing less than $10. There are hoards of financial advisors everywhere who would be more than happy to work up a financial profile for you. Some charge for this service. But be a bit cautious of this approach. The information is valuable, but financial planners tend to steer you into investment programs where they get a commission. They seldom suggest real estate because they don't sell it.

All planners are not equal. Ask lots of questions before you let anyone invest your money. If you're not comfortable, look elsewhere. The organizations that license the individual financial planners don't have the teeth to police what's going on in the field.

Whatever you consider investing in will depend on your comfort and experience level. You must seek the type of investments that will enable you to sleep at night. Be suspicious of anyone trying to offer you a deal with unrealistic returns. This should raise a big red flag. The "everybody-is-getting-in-on-this," or "friends', relatives', and those-in-the-know" deals should alert you to step aside.

Please don't sign up for something over the phone or from your front door. Whatever the investment, if it sounds too good to be true, it probably is. Ask yourself, why am I being asked to get into this deal? Great deals are kept in small groups. You don't want to become a statistic.

Try not to loan money to friends or relatives. If the professionals at the bank won't loan it to them, why should you? This could prevent huge sticky problems down the road. If you need to, don't loan it, just give someone the money. There will be fewer hassles later.

Don't ever forget whose money it is. There are many salespeople out there who will confuse you into thinking it's their money. It's not. You earn it, you control it.

I would encourage you first to set aside some of your money for your church and for charity. Individuals contribute 83% of the $130 billion donated to charity annually. This practice alone will return much to your life experience.

Almost everyone can and should save something. The problem is everything we own is tied to the magnetic account number at the bottom of your checks. Everything. Car, refrigerator, washer, dryer, dentist, pool pump, pets, everything. Once you think you have some extra money these things you own see it and promptly eat it up. But even if it's only a dollar a week, that's a start. The direction here is to place your money in a compound interest-bearing vehicle. Simply put, this is where your money will be working for you 24 hours per day, 365 days a year, even if you are sleeping or are on vacation. As Dr. Dennis E. Hensley illustrates in his book *Moneywise,* "If Columbus had put $1.00 into a passbook savings account earning 5% simple interest in 1492 when he came to America, today his account would be worth approximately $30.00. However, if he had put $1.00 into a passbook savings account that was paying 5% **compounded** interest, today his account would be worth more than $39 billion." That's **billion**! What a difference!

Dr. Hensley also responds to those who point to Scripture where it says the Lord takes care of the lilies in the field and the sparrow. They ask, "Won't He also take care of me?" "True," says Hensley, "but remember one thing: God doesn't throw the worms into the nest. You must do your part. I believe the Lord will throw down a rope. It's up to us to pull ourselves out."

Many people say their expenses are so high they can't save. If you kept track of all your expenses for one week, you would find areas where you could cut to save more.

In Jonathan Pond's book, *Safe Money in Tough Times,* he lists 101 ways to reduce expenses. A couple of ideas are: 1. Stop playing the lottery. 2. Brown-bag it at work. (This annual savings could be enough for a month's rent or a mortgage payment.) 3. Buy a water saver for your shower. 4. Raise the deductibles on your insurance.

Louis L'Amour wrote, "Victory is not won in miles but in

inches. Win a little now, hold your ground, and later win a little more."

You could open a Christmas Club account and not use the money for Christmas. I heard a fellow in Boston say he was able to get the down payment for his house in three years by using a Christmas Club account. You can have automatic transfers from your checking account to savings, mutual funds or other investments.

American Express has a plan where it will bill you between $50 and $5,000 a month extra on your credit card to go into a savings account. There is no penalty if you don't make the savings payment.

You can have money placed in your Credit Union savings by payroll deduction. Most people are so busy borrowing from their credit unions, they don't realize they can also save there. This is the "don't see it, don't miss it" form of savings. A Phoenix Hecht-Gallup poll found that 70% of consumers operated better under a forced savings arrangement.

Most people don't function well on a budget. Budgets are like diets. My definition of a diet is "an intense period just before weight gain." Don't practice the all-or-nothing. The secret here is balance. But instead of cars, stereos, boats, RV's, large screen TV's, trips and lots of clothes, lean toward gaining some savings and assets. If you establish and follow a realistic plan it won't take too long before you will be operating from a secure financial base and able to afford those personal desires. You can do both.

There are too many people who use the ostrich theory for their finances. They stick their heads in the sand and don't think the future is coming. The future arrives all too soon. Then they get to a point where they will outlive their assets and shortchange their lives at a time when they should be enjoying the fruits of their labors.

If you were planning on Social Security for a portion of your retirement, you should know that it will now only pay for about one week of your average monthly expenses. Plan now, enjoy later. It's not really that difficult.

Merrill Lynch surveyed 400 employed workers 45 to 64 years old. Fifty-nine percent expected their retirement money to come from Social Security and their company retirement plan. In reality only 35% would have their retirement income coming from those sources. That's a 24% error, one that would have a big impact on retirement. Planning for and having assets could be the parachute that breaks your fall during the times of financial uncertainty, illness or loss of your job.

 Most people don't plan to fail; they fail to plan.
—John L. Beckley

Whatever you do with your money will depend on you and your family's motivation. Remember, life is what happens to you when you are too busy to make plans. George Bernard Shaw said, "Success covers a multitude of blunders." Success is 80% skill and 20% luck and the help of the good Lord. If you are on the hike to the top of success, stop along the way and enjoy life. Because at the top there might be nothing; and 100% of nothing is nothing.

For the most part, money can't buy you health, happiness (if you're not already happy before you have money, don't expect a miracle), and real friendships. What money really buys you is **time**. Think about it. If you had enough money you could work less, if at all, and do whatever you desired.

There is no free lunch, but there are better places to eat.

Nugget: Complete a financial statement to know what shape you are in financially. Make up a plan with realistic goals within your budget. Start saving 5% to 10% of your after-tax income.

How: Follow your plan. It's not how much money you make. It's how much you get to keep legally.

 Shoot for the moon. Even if you miss it, you will land among the stars.
—Les Brown

There is much more to learn about money. Since I don't want to interrupt the flow of this book, I've placed more information in Appendix B at the back of the book. For instance, if you want to know more about credit cards, what's going on with your credit, needing money, buying a car, negotiating tips, working with your tax man, buying a home, 401K savings plans and a whole lot more, go to Appendix B.

Chapter 43

Variable Interest Rate

Because of those times, places, and things that carry us down the journey of life, the things that make us feel loved will sometimes change. Dating, children, work, play, age, divorce, desires, illness, and religion, to mention a few, can change our course in life. This process is the variable interest rate of the Love Bank.

It sometimes becomes necessary to do a periodic audit of the account because we want to get the best return possible on our investment (those Love Bank deposits we are making into the account). You don't need a broker to handle this task (they charge an annual fee). You just have to set the time aside and ask the question, "What are those things that make you feel special or loved?"

Nugget: Check the variable interest rate on the Love Bank Account.

How: Audit the Love Bank Account on a semi-annual basis, at least.

Chapter 44

✳ If You Don't Plan, You Won't Go

For your own mental health you must go away somewhere on a regular basis. But, if you don't plan, you won't go. Oh, I know, you can't go because of the kids, you don't have the money and your schedule is too full . . . that's a bunch of non-sense. Going away is not optional, it's mandatory.

If you planned it, you could find a trusted relative or friend who would take care of your kids if you choose to go away without them. You would find the money to go if even for a tank of gas and a day-trip to a nowhere adventure (sometimes these can be the best kinds). There is no alternative—you have to go.

You probably won't realize what a hectic pace you keep until you go away and then try to gear up again when you return. Remember, when they put you in the hole in the ground you don't come back. Not even for weekends. Don't get me wrong, Heaven is my home but I'm not homesick yet.

Well, you'll argue, there's this problem of my husband or wife, who never wants to go anywhere. If so, then it's time to sit down and negotiate some time away. If your spouse says it's not the money, it's probably the money. Other times, people are just homebodies. If your partner still won't go, consider taking separate vacations. You go away alone (or with a friend or relative) and your spouse can stay home. But don't be too surprised if you find that at the last minute the don't-go-won't-go person shows some interest in going. If he or she doesn't, however, then you go anyway. Bon Voyage!

Negotiating time also needs to be spent with the person who always plans or influences where you are going to go, based on his or her golf, fishing, tennis, relatives, bed & breakfast, shopping or other hobby and self-centered interests.

You're going to be dead a long time. The Bible says to be packed and ready to go at all times because you never know when you're going (you have noticed this, haven't you). Why not start enjoying what you have now before the long dirt nap? You deserve an adventure!

The time isn't right? Well, the time never seems to be right, does it? Just plan it and go for it. When you start planning, put the date on the calendar so you can anticipate **what's a comin'**. The great thing about getting away is the anticipation of going and the memories after. The only way to see and feel how you fit into this world is to get out and travel.

Many go away with a hidden agenda to work out pent-up problems in their relationships that they haven't had the time, skills or participation from their partner to resolve. This has ruined many a trip when it has been sprung on the unsuspecting partner.

Ann was finally getting to go on a vacation to Acapulco with Tom. After two children and a lot of unresolved issues, she stated this was his last chance to save their relationship. He didn't have a clue. If they couldn't work out their problems it was over. Nothing had changed except they were going on vacation.

If you are planning on trying to use your vacation to fix your relationship, you are going for the wrong reasons. If you can't work it out before you go or agree that this will be the time to do it, leave this baggage at home.

Don't just plan one trip. Get into the habit of planning and going. Simply lock in the dates on the calendar and watch what happens. Adopt the philosophy that if you're not already on a trip, you're planning the next one.

A Gallup poll found some interesting facts about how Americans want their vacations to be.

- Almost two-thirds said the most important reason for a vacation was to relax, reduce stress, rest, take a break or escape.

- Fifty-five percent of Americans are taking shorter (a week or less), more frequent vacations, probably a reflection of their two-income lifestyles. More than half of all Americans in this category take at least two vacations.

- Eighty-six percent of parents said a vacation with the kids is more "fun" than "drudgery."

- Women are much more ready to go away without the kids or hubby.

- Over half of the travelers preferred active sight-seeing vacations over sedentary ones.

So, where are you going? Some people get stuck in a rut as to where to go to get away. They end up going to the same old theme parks they have been to before. The only difference between a rut and a grave is the depth. My friend Dennis and his family have been to Disneyland umpteen times. In desperation they end up going because they won't plan and venture out to the full spectrum of opportunities available for places to go. They charge down Highway 5 for the six-plus hours drive on a Friday, endure the long lines, heat and smog, and drag home on Sunday frustrated and exhausted. They end up amazed at what has happened: as educated and intelligent people, they have been foolish enough to have done the same vacation again. Dennis told me recently that they had booked a new vacation this year. Where do you think they are going? Disneyworld—in August. No heat, humidity, or crowds then!

So where do you want to go? There are plays, musicals, fairs, festivals and special season events everywhere.

Every community seems to have an annual entertainment book that is sold by Little League, soccer teams, school bands and church organizations. They offer two meals for the price of one at numerous restaurants, and discounts on everything from rental cars to dance lessons. They are an excellent investment that can be used for creative dating or just to get you out to get the smell of the city blown off of you.

The Sunday papers are full of ideas worldwide or right in your area. One recent section I saw was dedicated to Summer By the Bay. This showed upcoming events in cities of the San Francisco Bay area. Another article was on how to travel like a tightwad. A revised touring production of "Bye Bye Birdie" was sold out in San Francisco. But by checking the Sunday entertainment section, we saw that they were adding a matinee. A quick call produced second-row center seats for a great afternoon of the revised classic followed by dinner in the city.

Everyone loves a bargain. Depending on how hard you want to work for a trip that fits your travel budget will determine what you'll end up with. Some people don't need a bargain. They can afford to just go if they would only plan a vacation . . . and follow through and take it.

If you can pretend you have gone away (although you're still at home), you can expand your horizons at home. Think about it. When you're on a trip you are more laid back, in better spirits. As a tourist, you take off to explore museums, hang out with the Romans at the cafes, check out the night life and take long walks. It's all a change of attitude. You can adopt this same changed attitude at home. With it you can meet new friends, take in events, try new restaurants and places to visit.

It might be as much fun and as easy as finding out why people come to your area to vacation. There are probably a number of places you have never been to in your own back yard. Go to hotels in your area and pick up travel brochures of those sightseeing things to do right in your home town. If there is a tour available, take it. You could find out a lot of what you didn't know about your locale.

There is camping or renting a camping trailer.

You don't need to own a recreational vehicle where you have to pay the insurance, storage and installments all year long. You can rent one to take the whole family away, including the dog. We took an RV trip up the Redwood Highway in California, along the rugged Oregon Coast into beautiful Washington State. There we went by ferry to Victoria, British Columbia, the Butchart Gardens and back into Vancouver, Canada. We stopped when and where we wanted to accommodate our schedule and interests.

🔥 *Go First Class once in awhile . . . because your heirs will.*

Amtrak has some great travel packages. Our family went from San Jose, California to San Luis Obispo by train on a weekend package that included a room and a first class tour of Hearst Castle.

There is an overabundance of hotel rooms and suites available nationwide or within easy driving distance from your home. These bargains can provide a great getaway. Many offer weekend specials that extend a weekend into Monday. A weekend getaway was the #1 way to show romance for women on a Roper survey. In order to obtain your best deal follow these simple rules:

1. Don't call on the 800 reservation number. Call direct to the hotel you want to stay at during the day when the "A" team is on. The day manager and crew know the current best deal.

2. The standard rate for a room is called the rack rate. Many don't pay this price and neither should you. Don't settle for a miserly 5% or 10% off. If they say the room is $175, say, "I was thinking about $90. What can you do for me?"

3. Be as flexible as possible about the date. This allows you to take advantage of up to 50% off and/or a second night free.

4. Ask what the corporate rate is. Yes, your life experience entitles you to the corporate rate. Your last name is your corporation. They won't ask when you arrive to verify your corporation. The corporate rate might not be the best rate, though. Ask about specials. Recently, I called a hotel to reserve a night at an airport before a trip. I was given the standard rate. I asked for and was quoted the corporate rate. I asked if that was their best rate. She said, "That's our corporate rate." "Yes, but is that your best rate?" A pause at the other end, then, "No, our best rate is $20 less."

5. Ask if anything else comes with the room. In the above situation, the room came with a full breakfast, free parking while we were gone for two weeks, and a shuttle to the airport.

6. Ask if there are any specials being offered. When we were going on a college tour with our son Stu, one of our stops was going to be Santa Barbara. I had made a reservation at a modest motel, but on a lark I called the Santa Barbara Biltmore (where we stayed on a previous trip). I asked what the rate was and was quoted $190-250 per night. I asked, "Is there a Sunday night special?" "One moment, I'll check." She came back on the line and said, "Why, yes, there is. It's $90." Sold. When we arrived they put us in a large front unit like a suite. They even brought in an exercise rowing machine for our son.

When you ask if there are any specials, the reservation person might not have one, but once they check the occupancy rate and see that it's too low, all of a sudden there is a new special rate for you. If you don't get any satisfaction, ask for the supervisor or manager. Whenever you obtain a special rate, get the person's first and last name who agreed to your deal. When you arrive at the hotel, ask if there are any additional specials that have occurred since you made your reservation.

This proved valuable for us on a stay at the fabulous Willard Hotel in Washington, DC. We had booked a great weekend special. But, we also wanted to stay there Monday night. We went all the way to the Manager without getting anyone to budge on the standard rate for the Monday stay. When we arrived at the Willard, Harriet went in to register while I took care of the car and luggage. Harriet just asked, "Now, what is the rate going to be for Monday?"

The reply was, "Oh, we have just added a summer extravaganza." The rate was 50% off the rate we were quoted for Monday night. And only $5.00 more than the weekend nightly special. Ask and ye shall receive.

We called a hotel in San Francisco during the Christmas season and asked if they had a Christmas shoppers' special. You know, they did. The rate was $80 off. The stores in this Union Square location also had a special of wrapping your presents and delivering them back to your room. The royal treatment. What a country!

Do you know hotels have a day rate? Most do. It's usually used by business people to freshen up and rest during a travel and business schedule. You can use this day rate, too. Be sure to bargain for the best rate.

We've been known to go on a mini escape to the five star Clift Hotel in San Francisco on the day rate. We go to lunch, back to the room for a nap, then conversation, champagne, a little romance, showers, get dressed for dinner and out of the room by about 6 p.m. (this time can be flexible) for less than half of the regular discounted room rate. After dinner in the city we go home refreshed. This is really creative dating.

Discount Travel Clubs and Tourist Bureaus

It's sometimes possible to get a travel package for the price of the airfare alone. Many tourist bureaus, travel agents and travel clubs offer these bargains. Be sure to secure these trips with a credit card to protect your investment on your trip if a problem arises with the travel agency. In addition to having a crackerjack travel agent, we belong to Preferred Travel Club: (800) 638-0930. We have an 800 number that keeps us informed on what is available for cruises, airfares, hotels, tour packages and specials. We also have an international listing of hotels and villas that offer discounts, with some offering the second and seventh night free. Vacations To Go in Houston, at (800) 338-4962, offers similar service.

Most airlines have internet web sites with last minute discounts for business travelers or vacation travel locations. Here are a few web site addresses (URL's):

www.Americanair.com—Recent fare Chicago-Los Angeles for $189.

www.bestfares.com—Site features hidden travel deals.

www.travelweb.com—Site features click-it weekend deals.

When we visited our son Stuart at college, we stayed at a Residence Inn for $30 off the discount rate.

There are several cruise lines offering last-minute getaway cruises. You might find yourself being whisked off on a bargain cruise and having your cabin upgraded in the process. And about cruises—they are not for the overfed, newly wed and nearly dead anymore. Carnival Cruise Lines claims 70% of their passengers are under age 55. You don't need that extensive, expensive wardrobe anymore. You can dress as elaborately as you like, but it's not mandatory. Cruises offer the convenience of being in an air conditioned hotel near a number of faraway ports of call where you only unpack one time. They have family packages to keep everyone interested. With more and larger cruise ships coming on line, fly-cruise packages will remain low in price. Most cruise lines will even match up singles. Many ships have escorts to dance with, play cards, and who comfort older single passengers. Don't expect the Love Boat. The last cruise we were on there were six single women to each man. One thing you will find out by taking a cruise, more suicides are committed with a knife and a fork than any other weapon. The food is fabulous! The chefs will prepare any special meals you prefer.

Our first cruise was to the Caribbean. The change to an instant rich diet upset my system. This, combined with the humid climate, produced a chafed area bottomside. I went through our vanity case and found a jar of Vitamin E lotion. I applied it to the affected area that afternoon and evening without improvement. After a shower the next morning, I began to apply another treatment, but Harriet saw me and yelled, "What are you doing?"

I said, "I'm applying this Vitamin E lotion where I hurt."

She said, "That's not Vitamin E lotion, that's Woolite. I brought it to wash things in the sink."

Try not to get caught up in the frenzy of non-stop activities on any trip. Many people who travel think, "well, we've paid the money and I'm going to get as much out of this trip as I can." (I know a guy who set his alarm clock on a cruise so he could get up and take advantage of the midnight buffet.) They become the kamikaze travelers on jet lag. They get to a point where they need a vacation from the vacation. Some people come back from a trip exhausted. Aren't you going away to relax?

You know that long list you make up of things to do or see that everyone tells you about when you're planning your trip? (They all have been there and are instant experts.) Well, just before you get on the plane, throw it away. You'll never be able to do all those things.

Here's a good rule of thumb for packing for a trip. Just before you leave take out half the clothes and take twice as much money. It will work out just about right. My brother and his wife were going away alone on their first vacation to Hawaii for seven days. They were taking five suitcases. Yes, five trunks. They had sweaters, coats and first aid supplies. They looked like they were going on a three-month safari. It's a rule with us that if you want to bring it, you get to carry it.

On a family trip to Hawaii (big mistake in taking your kids to Hawaii—every time you want to go again, so do they) as we were loading up to head for the airport, our eldest son Rob said, "Well, I guess it's time to go pack." He was serious. In less than five minutes he was ready. He said, "What do you need anyway for Hawaii: two pairs of shorts, a couple of tops and sandals." (He really took more.)

Don't worry about what you might forget to bring. Just buy it there.

We feel fortunate to have had the opportunity to expose our children to traveling. We feel it has enriched their lives. On a family trip to the Garden Isle of Kauai, Hawaii, our son Rob invited his darling Nancy. They hiked back along the Napali Coast to a secluded waterfall where he asked her to marry him. They feel they now have a special place in this world to return to someday. The acorn doesn't fall too far from the tree.

There are trips with customized options, where you can book have-it-your-way vacation trips with pre-set prices. These mass customizations are fast, flexible and affordable. Hyatt Resorts and others are offering exclusive inclusive packages that allow a couple to vary the plans for the same price. He can do the spa while she does tennis, golf, or horseback riding. There are complete one-set-price packages at dude ranches that give families full options together or supervised children's activities so Mom and Dad can ride off alone for awhile. This is not like the brochure for the movie "City Slickers." You don't have the hassle of making all the plans here. You just show up for horseback rides, river rafting, square dancing, hayrides and fishing, or do nothing but relax by the pool and eat chuck wagon good grub. When our kids were growing up, we spent many good times and have fond memories of the M-BAR-J Guest Ranch in the Sierra foothills. We felt like family with Archie and Bunny at this quasi-rustic working ranch.

🔥 *Sit loosely in the saddle of life.*
–Robert Louis Stevenson (1850–1894)

We took a "Taulk" fall colors tour through the New England states. This was a no name tag, open menu leisure trip. The all-inclusive trip wasn't just the brilliant colors, it was the history. Starting in Boston (yes, we went to Cheers), we were at the North Church where the signal "one if by land and two if by sea" was sent. Next, we were on the road with Paul Revere to Lexington where the shot was fired that was heard around the world. Then to Concord and Walden Pond. Things we had read about all our lives came to life. These were exciting and emotional times.

And don't feel that just because you haven't planned, you don't have anywhere to go except that same old theme park at the last minute. Even the hot spots could have a room at the Inn, maybe at a discount because they're not full at this late date. Just pick up the phone and call, instead of lying out in the wading pool in the backyard feeling depressed. Don't forget to bargain. Delta Airlines has cut-rate bargains you can book to Hawaii, Mexico and the Caribbean Islands up to 48 hours prior to departure, with no higher rate penalties for airfare and room. Call Delta at (800) 872-7786.

Delta, and other airlines also have fly/drive packages where it would be too far to drive. One destination is Branson, Missouri, the country music center.

If you are too busy, try calling a consolidator. They buy blocks of rooms and airline bookings at a discount and pass on big savings to you. By calling (800) 96-Hotel you can get a $190 room in San Francisco for $89 a night. For a complete package at Disneyland/Disneyworld call (800) 511-5321.

There are travel packages for singles, there is a growing market for parents traveling with their adult children, and the flourishing women-only journeys. Try Smart Woman Traveler (800) 250-8428 or Maiden Voyages at (800) 528-8425.

> 🔥 *Men tend to be much more destination oriented. "Get there, do that, get back." Women want to mosey along and digest the place.*
> **—Mary Clark, Smart Woman Traveler**

By mid-August many travel destinations, especially London and Europe, and most airlines offer cheap discounts if seats haven't been reserved. They would rather book a discount than go empty.

Whatever you have an interest in doing on a getaway or vacation, just plan it, follow through with it and go. Be prepared to surrender, especially if your luggage gets lost, or your room isn't what you expected or is not ready when you arrive. On a trip to Waikiki I was upset because our room wasn't ready at check-in time or half an hour later when we checked again. That was, until I found out they were upgrading us to a suite with a panoramic view of Waikiki Beach and Diamond Head smack dab out our window. Well, okay then! We didn't want to leave the room. Sometimes our luck turns out to be better than the best laid plans.

Traveling with Friends

Go on a small outing first before planning a large vacation with friends or relatives, especially if they're bringing their kids. Otherwise you might ruin a good friendship by going together. People have such varied interests and desires that it is difficult to coordinate who wants to see and do **what**, much less where are we going to eat? Isn't half the fun of going away meeting new friends and just relaxing by yourselves? If you simply must go together, book separate rooms for sure. A second car (for the kids, too) could free up everyone's schedule.

Nugget: If you don't plan, you won't go. Don't just plan the trips. You must also follow through and go on them. Plan more than one trip at a time. Put the planned trip on the calendar to anticipate what's-a-comin'.

How: Invest a little time to find the right trips and adventures that will interest you and fit your budget. Newspaper travel sections and USA Today will keep you current on airline fares and available trips. Get a crackerjack travel agent on your team.

Plan your escape.
—"Captain Bob"

Personal Experience by Barry

I was supposed to take my sons (I'm divorced) on a trip to Disneyland. The plans suddenly changed and I needed to leave the next day. A quick check with a travel agent produced airline costs that would have cancelled the trip. I called Southwest Airlines (they're not in the travel agents' reservation system). Not only did I get the best airfare, I got a free ticket for one of my boys on a special offer. How about a car? I called Dollar Rental Car about their advertised special and got an upgrade because I was flying with Southwest Airlines. Where do we stay? I called a hotel where we stayed before. Once I was quoted the rack rate I followed the procedures to get my best rate. By the time we ended, I got the room for $69 including a full breakfast.

Personal Experience by Dennis

I was a bit discouraged that I hadn't planned enough in advance to take my family to Monterey/Carmel, California for the weekend. I called a few places including where we had stayed before, but they were all full. Then I called Resort To Me at (408) 646-9250. I was surprised to find out they had several options available. We decided on a special at Carmel Valley Ranch. It would be $165 for the five of us for the weekend. This included tennis, swimming, and optional golf and horseback riding.

Nancy's Trip

In July, my wife Harriet invited our daughter-in-law Nancy to go with her to visit relatives in North Carolina. The week-long trip was being scheduled for the following March. Nancy declined because she was still nursing Christian and couldn't see leaving three-year-old Trevor at home with his dad. But four months later, Christian was done nursing. She started thinking that a week away would be great, especially if she didn't have to take the boys. Like many women, however, Nancy felt guilty about leaving her young children even though her husband was capable of taking care of the kids.

Nancy came to me, torn over the decision and pressuring herself to bring at least one of the boys if she did go. She asked me, "What should I do?" I said, "Ruunnnnn, Nancy! Rob has the time off and I'll help him while you're gone. Go!"

Nancy spent a relaxing week touring between relatives in a part of the country she had never seen. It was spring. The dogwood was in bloom. They fed her real well. Did she feel guilty? Yes, at first. She got over it quickly. She deserved this trip. Nancy is glad she went, because she got a chance to know one of the relatives who has since passed away.

Boy, was it hard work taking care of a toddler and a preschooler! It never ended. I now have a greater respect for mothers. Rob has a whole different appreciation for his wife, as does Nancy for her husband.

After I told this story at a mothers club presentation, I got this note: "My aunt has invited me to go on a cruise this summer. I've felt guilty just thinking about going, even though my husband said it's OK. Now I know I'm going. Signed—Bon Voyage, Joyce."

If you don't plan, you won't go!

This is the last chapter for the condensed version of this book. I didn't include Chapter 37 ("Sex and Other Stuff") in the condensed version, since I thought you would be curious enough to read it anyway. The chapters in this book are Nuggets for communication and relationships. You can reach in any drawer of the tool box (read any chapter) or grab the next Nugget that interests you. Each one is a recipe to mix up and sweeten the quality of your life.

Chapter 45

Be Serendipitous

You have heard the word serendipity, but do you know its meaning? It comes from a Persian fable. There were three princes from Serendip who set out to find a treasure. Although they never found the treasure, they had so many great experiences along the way that their experiences were worth far more than locating the treasure. A serendipitous event, then, is one of those great, unusual and unexpected experiences that we stumble upon in life.

You can only find these treasures by getting out of the homebody aspects of your lifestyle and on to journeys that produce serendipitous treasures. They're everywhere. You can be a spontaneous serendip prince or princess for yourself and your family.

My wife and I took an unplanned vacation one year. Without any reservations we set off to go up the "Forty-Niner Gold" Highway 49 in California, starting at Grass Valley, a point we had never previously ventured beyond. This was rather uncomfortable for me because I always want to be in control of where we are going and what we do, and know where we are going to bed down at night. I need to have everything packaged and boxed up instead of just going out to find the serendipities. However, I had been missing great treasures because of my lack of spontaneity.

Up the Forty-Niner Highway we went. Our first stop was

the quaint gold town of Downeyville. Dredges were still work-ing in the rivers and streams. "There's still gold in them 'thar hills," I assured my wife. Walking around the side streets, we stopped to talk with an old-timer about the past. Once a deputy sheriff, he had seen the changes. He knew all about claim jumping, severe winters, hangings and stretching the truth with folklore.

We lucked out and found a room in the Helm's St. Charles Bed and Breakfast in Goodyear's Bar: (530) 289-0910. This was an original 1864 stagecoach stop with some of the original antique furniture. Breakfast the next morning was prepared on the wood stove in the kitchen where Tammy served us a full meal starting with fresh baked jam scones. Husband Mark told stories of the Goodbar's gold strike, the storm of 1870 that tilted the west wall of the hotel, and finding rare coins and tools during restoration.

Over the hill past Sierra City and down the east side of the Sierra Nevada range were pristine alpine lakes like Sardine, Salmon and Gold. We went through Graeagle, to the town of Quincy. There we stumbled upon a fiddle festival and a local theatrical group performing the play "Woo Done It."

While in Quincy we asked about accommodations at Mount Lassen Volcanic National Park, our next stop. We were told of a secluded lodge, seventeen miles from Chester, deep into the National Park on a dead end road. Normally, you can't get a room there because they sometimes have a two-year wait for reservations. We called anyway and found they were, indeed, booked. When we went through Chester we saw the road sign for the lodge and we decided to visit anyway, for future reference.

The road went to dirt the last three miles. Then we came upon the secluded hundred-year-old lodge settled in a spec-

tacular meadow. When we were checking on rates and avail-
ability for the following year the manager said, "Do you want
to stay now?"

"What? Really?"

"Yes, we have had a cancellation. Would you like to see
the room?"

"Why, yes." It was a step back in time as we walked up the
creaking stairs and down the hall to Room #6. There were no
outside locks on the door. As we opened up the door to the
room in this rustic lodge the only light was a kerosene lamp.
The only electricity was in the dining hall, provided by a gen-
erator. We could hear the distant sound of a stream, and a gentle breeze was blowing in through the window. There were no
televisions, radios or newspapers. There was only one phone
for the lodge—number two on a party line with nine other
parties. If your caller didn't know that he needed to go through
the Susanville operator, he could never find you.

There were hikes, optional horseback rides, a pool fed by a
hot spring from the volcanic activity in the area. There were
tall pines and Sequoia trees along the Pacific Crest Trail that
runs from Canada to Mexico, and huge puffy clouds overhead.
Since this was a serendipity trip, we had no plans and no reservations for anywhere else. I looked at Harriet and said, "We
would be fools not to stay."

This area was the home of Ishi, the last known Indian to
walk out of the wilderness in 1911. I read his story in this setting and identified the creeks and mountain peaks he knew. It
was an enriching experience. We have been returning every
year since to find peace in the meadow. We have become
friends with other families. It's like a family reunion. We don't
consider ourselves outdoor people. But this place has just the
right mix of people with varied interests, family activities,

great food, box lunches for heading out on hikes in the park, and a chance to simply relax by the pool. This is not an E-ticket ride. When you head home it's like Ishi coming out of the wilderness back to civilization.

During our first visit we climbed to the peak of Mount Lassen. From the top you can see up and down the Sierra and Cascade mountain ranges. Had we not taken that first unscheduled trip, we wouldn't have experienced all these serendipitous situations.

Nugget: The world is full of serendipitous experiences for you to discover off the beaten path or right in your own backyard.

How: Be spontaneous.

Personal Experience by Susan

We had made plans with two young women to go to the top of the tram at Squaw Valley. We wanted to ice skate in the new year-round outdoor ice skating rink in July. When we got to the tram we found out the ice rink was closed. We decided to go up anyway in order to show our friends the view and to go for a hike.

Our serendipity was finding a large patch of snow on a hill. Now, being the playful one that I am given credit for being, I began to slide down the hill, first on my feet, then on my ski jacket. Everyone joined in. It was great fun. It turned into an unexpected white frosty surprise in July.

After several slides and much laughter we had forgotten about the ice skating rink being closed, so we indulged in a happy, unplanned snow discovery on the mountain.

Personal Experience by Helen

We were staying in the fishing village of Erciere just up the coast from Lisbon, Portugal. One morning while we were watching the fishing fleet unload, the fish auction started. The large boxes of assorted seafood were each given a number. The auctioneer, accompanied by a policeman, started the bidding. The bids started high and gradually were reduced. When a price was right, someone bid by making a hissing sound. Many of the hefty women walked away with huge boxes of slippery fish balanced on their heads. They were each given a slip of paper noting the sale. A fishy credit card?

I told Jack that I knew the bidding was made by a hissing sound and proceeded to demonstrate. He said, "Be careful or we'll be paying for a box of flounders that you'll have to balance on your head."

Personal Experience by Debbie

I went from my home in Illinois to visit relatives in California. Since my last name is so unusual I always check names in the phone book when I'm in a new area, trying to locate possible distant relatives. While on a side trip to San Jose I found a person in the phone book with my last name. I wrote to him and got a reply. By coincidence, our mothers had the same first name. As we continued to correspond we found that our mothers were from the same town. What I came to find out was that this was my older **brother!** He had been adopted at an early age and no one was told the story. I now write to *my* brother on a regular basis. Our families get together at an annual picnic.

I not only found a brother I didn't know about, but a new set of nieces, nephews and other relatives I didn't know existed.

Chapter 46

Wedding Colors

In the process of gaining information to write this book I did an informal survey of girls and young women aged twelve to eighteen. I first asked them if they had thought about getting married at some point. Most had. The surprise came when I asked if they had selected the colors for their wedding. More than 90% of them could tell me the colors and other details about their wedding.

While hiking up to Yosemite Falls we came across a group of youngsters. I asked two twelve-year old girls from Sacramento about their wedding plans. They beamed with excitement about the colors they had already selected. The young boys and the dads in their group were bewildered.

It should be no surprise why young women know about their wedding colors and plans for their weddings. Just look at a young girl's bedroom. As youngsters they dress up as flower girls and they are bridesmaids in the weddings of friends and family members. They try to catch the bride's bouquet. (There is a board game on the market called, "Here Comes the Bride.") A friend told me he had just attended a wedding where the young bride announced that she had been receiving *Bride's* magazine for the previous ten years in preparation for her wedding.

On the national evening news a few years ago there was a woman in her early thirties on the East coast who was so intent on her wedding that when her suitor did not show up she had a mock wedding, complete with her wedding dress, cake, the reception with friends and relatives, a band and throwing the bouquet. She said she had waited and saved so long for her wedding that even though the required groom didn't appear, she wasn't going to be cheated out of the experience. As such, instead of just going on a vacation, she had a wedding.

As Lord Byron wrote in *Don Juan*, "Man's love is of man's life a thing apart; 'tis woman's whole existence."

If I know a guy who is in the process of getting married, I'll ask him if the bride-to-be has cried yet. They'll usually look surprised and say, "How did you know?" or "Let me count the times and ways."

If you are a guy getting married here's the complete list of all you need to do:

1. Almost nothing. Stay out of the way.
2. Don't keep saying, "Whatever you want dear." You have to really care about whatever it is you're supposed to care about.
3. Wear a white shirt without ruffles.
4. Don't sing at the reception.
5. Pick a best man who has something humorous to say already prepared.

That's it! You will never understand that this is the day that your love has been waiting for years. The wedding is not about you. It is for your bride-to-be, her mother and yours, their mothers, any other women in the family, and all their lady friends. That's why they dress guys only in tuxedos. If the groom doesn't work out, the other guys in line just take one step forward. The next guy is dressed and ready to go. Almost anyone will do.

This is serious business. Just stay out of the way. The women have all the etiquette down. You must keep showing up at all the meetings and act interested or she will cry again. If you run over budget, just keep bringing more money. If you mess this up you will be in the penalty box doing hard time for a long, long time.

A few thoughts for the bride:

1. Try to marry someone you love.
2. Use K.I.S.S. Keep it Simple Sweetie.
3. Spend most of the money on your dress and good champagne. You don't want to be referred to as the bride in the frumpy dress, or that wedding with the cheap champagne that gave me a headache.
4. Don't do anything funny with your hair. This is not the senior ball. You want the groom to recognize you.
5. Don't wear a hat.
6. Personalize the wedding by having the reception at home. It will be more relaxing.
7. The wedding cake should be a traditional white cake.
8. Listen to everything your mothers says, then do what you want.
9. Your mother can do no wrong on the wedding day.

Weddings can be emotional experiences, especially for women. (I cry at weddings, too.) To renew the emotions, feelings and the vows of marriage, attend weddings. The different surroundings and excitement can boost the wedding colors of your own marriage.

Here is a letter I wrote to my son Rob after his wedding:

My Dear Son Rob:

What a special time it was at your wedding. Although I knew it was coming, I was taken aback with being a proud parent and seeing you take the step.

Rob, I was totally overwhelmed by the love you were showing to your bride. You were saying sweet things, in your own way, in her ear, caressing her, cooing and showing genuine love and affection.

I will never forget your display of love.

I love you,

Your Father (the dad)

Nugget: Accept wedding invitations. Don't bypass the ceremony and go directly to the reception.

How: RSVP

A True Story from Fantasy Land

When Stu was five years old, he told his mother he wanted to marry her and go live in the castle at Disneyland. During college, his rock climbing experience enabled him to work part-time as a character at Disneyland climbing the Matterhorn. He became sweethearts with Wendy, who was also a character at Disneyland. Eventually, it became serious. It was time to pop the question. Stu caught Wendy in costume on her break at Disneyland. On one knee, Stu asked "Minnie Mouse" to marry him. Minnie's high-pitched voice answered, "Yes."

It's not the original story Stu told when he was five . . . but close enough.

Chapter 47

Flower Therapy

My friend Vern told me recently about going into a florist shop to order some flowers. As he was looking through the cards to attach to his arrangement, he noticed a card that showed a guy crawling out of a dog house. He asked the owner, "Is this a joke?" The owner replied, "Nope, that's my fastest moving signature card."

Too many men turn to flowers only when they're in trouble, which is probably not the best time to give flowers. This sends the wrong message. Flowers mean "I'm in trouble."

While in a florist shop recently, I mentioned this trouble/flowers connection to the owner. The guy next to me said, "Yeah, if I brought flowers home my wife would think something was wrong."

This became perfectly clear to me once when I was in the dog house. (It was probably my fault, too.) I figured I could just cruise down to the florist shop and buy my way out of trouble. I purchased a beautiful colorful arrangement in a vase, marched home and made my presentation, which I thought would smooth things over. Wrong! Ten minutes later I found the arrangement out by the garbage can.

A perfect opportunity is often lost here. A recent Roper romance survey found that the women surveyed listed long stem roses second as a sign of romance and any other bouquet was fourth on the survey.

How about giving flowers when we're not in trouble?

We live in one of the few countries where people do not send flowers regularly. But I feel we should. Flowers are wonderful. They convey feelings, color, warmth.

🔥 *Flowers always leave a fragrance in the hand that bestows them.*
–Chinese proverb

I really learned to enjoy and appreciate flowers once I figured out the appropriate way to give them. It doesn't have to be a special occasion. Flowers are easily available not only from a florist shop but also from many supermarkets and discount flower stands.

But you want to find out what flowers your partner doesn't like. Debbie is a teller where we bank. She has told her husband of eighteen years that she doesn't like roses. She especially doesn't like red roses. Guess what she was surprised with on her fortieth birthday? Forty red roses! Talk about not being heard.

The reward (the interest and dividend) in the Love Bank is high for the few dollars and the minimum effort involved in picking up some flowers. I've even been known to send flowers to my wife with a card that said, "For absolutely no reason except that I love you."

And flowers aren't just for women. I've received flowers. I've seen them delivered to men at work for promotions and other occasions.

When I do bring home or order flowers, I don't always get them in an arrangement with a vase. There seems to be a special excitement and ritual with women in cutting and arranging the flowers themselves. I have yet to find a workplace where a vase doesn't appear, probably from a vase heaven, when flowers show up.

My friend Dennis and I had been conducting business with a firm and had received great service from the secretary, Laurie. On the way over to the firm's office, I stopped and selected a bouquet of flowers. Dennis asked why I didn't just get an arrangement, that there probably wouldn't be a vase at the firm. I said, "Wait, you'll see." The flowers were a big hit. Right then, the flower ritual started. A vase appeared (from the vase fairy). The flowers were cut, arranged, the ribbon wrapped around the vase, and the card and holder were put in place. Any questions Dennis?

When someone has just had a baby, we wait about a week after Mom has returned home from the hospital before we send flowers. This is usually about the time the post partum blues set in. Many a time we hear back, "How did you know?"

My friend Vern made a perfect presentation when he first started dating his wife-to-be. On Valentine's Day he showed up at the school where she teaches. He was dressed in his Fire Department Class A dress uniform complete with white gloves and a **huge bouquet of roses.** Vern called Dayna out of the classroom and gave her the flowers. He says the best part was as he walked away and Dayna went back into the room, he could hear the roar of excitement from the students. Dayna and Vern are married and have two children.

Valentine's Day

Valentine's Day is one of the most important holidays for many women. Some men just don't get it. For them it's like trying to get women excited about Super Bowl Sunday. There are many guys who have this one figured out. Some guys though think it's just another day for them to mess up. Many think it's just another Hallmark holiday, a conspiracy by the card and flower folks.

One year, during the week of Valentine's day, a guy was in my wife's office making repairs. The gals in the office asked him if he knew what important holiday was that week? He didn't. When they told him, he said, "Yeah, I know, Valentine's Day is between Christmas and summer." He said, "I would have known in a day or so anyway because I'm on a guys' hot-line. We have been in so much trouble in the past that we formed this guys' phone hot line. If one of the members becomes aware of an event of importance, he calls the rest of the guys." This could have national significance.

If you want to see a pathetic sight, go into a florist after 3:00 p.m. on Valentine's Day. There will be a hoard of men milling around bumping into each other, completely out of their element. They waited until the last minute again, charged in, waited in long lines, paid a high price, and probably did not get their first choice of the flowers they wanted because they waited too long—again. But these guys know if they don't go home with flowers, their sweetheart is going to have the oven door open, the gas on, and her head inside.

My friend, Gene, told me a Valentine's story from last year. A couple of days before the special day, his wife Sharon said, "You bought me flowers last week; you don't need to get me flowers on Valentine's Day." That's not what she meant. Because when Gene came home without flowers, Sharon said, "All my girl friends got flowers." Gene stood there like Forest Gump and said, "Well, you told me not to do it." He went right out and got some flowers. Of course, then it was too late.

We celebrated our twenty-fifth wedding anniversary by going by train from Vancouver to Lake Louise, Canada. When I tried to order roses for the occasion the florist asked if I knew what I was doing. Long stem red roses in Canada are not easy to get and *if* you can get them, they're expensive. Whatever it took, this was part of my plan. Luckily, I was prepared when I got the Visa bill at home the next month. It was worth it.

I was considering substituting two of the roses with carnations. I was going to tell Harriet those were for those two bad years, you remember. But better judgment prevailed.

On that magic day I got into a tizzy because the 25 roses hadn't showed up. A check with the florist revealed they had made an error in our hotel location. Quick on their feet, they asked, "What restaurant are you going to? Great! We will deliver the flowers there."

As soon as we walked into the restaurant you could see the huge arrangement of long stem red roses. (I get chills just writing about this.) Talk about Love Bank deposits.

We received warm greetings from those in the restaurant. It actually turned out better than if they had been delivered to our room.

We did take the arrangement back to our room. When we left, Harriet gave the roses to the staff at the hotel. Since roses were not available in this area they were a big hit again. Harriet dried one that she keeps with a picture taken at the table in the restaurant.

When I first met Mike he was dating a true love. But Joyce ended the relationship because she thought Mike was too silly and immature. This hurt Mike deeply.

For the next seven years Mike patiently sent Joyce flowers anonymously on a regular basis.

Finally at a party one night they saw each other again. Not silly anymore (probably more mature), Mike was able to get a date and the relationship was rekindled.

Once the situation started to show signs of getting serious

Mike told Joyce that he had been the one who had faithfully been sending the flowers. Joyce emotionally fell apart. They are married and have a son. Love and flowers conquer all.

Tony is a firefighter and friend. He has a great imagination, is creative and he's a real romantic. When he started dating, they became true-to-life love birds. Wedding bells were sure to chime. When it came time to pop the question, Tony didn't want to do it in the traditional way. He took Joyce to Kauai, Hawaii. They went out scuba diving. Since Tony was a more experienced diver he went down first to check the area out then came back for Joyce. While on the dive, Tony pointed to a sea shell sitting on a rock. He signaled for Joyce to open it. What do you think was inside? The engagement ring she had been waiting for. She lost her mouth piece when she gasped and took in the whole ocean. Did she accept? . . . Well of course she did.

They married. The next year Joyce became pregnant with their first child. Then three months later Joyce was diagnosed with cancer. She held off as much of the treatment as possible until the baby was far enough along where labor could be induced. Jason was a little fighter and made it just fine. As much of a fighter as Joyce was, she couldn't beat this one. She passed away six months later.

Firefighters are a close family. Being so close, it affected all of us walking Tony and Joyce through this tragedy. After going through this ordeal, here he was with his emotions and a new child to raise. Friends and relatives pitched in to shore Tony up and help him get on with his life. There was no doubt he was anxious and depressed.

One of those who came forward was an old girlfriend Betty. As the volunteers pared off and got back to their lives, Betty remained. The caring schoolteacher grew attached to

Jason. Tony explained to her that he was emotionally in no position to be in a relationship. Betty understood. She was there to nurture. As time went on they did date. Tony repeated his emotional statement. A year-and-a-half passed. Jason was now two-and-a-half. A few days before Valentine's Day, Jason was sitting at the table eating. He held his little cup up to Betty and for the first time uttered these words, "Mommy, more."

Who do you think sent flowers to Betty at her school a few days later? The card read, "Thank you for being a good mommy to me." Signed Jason. Wedding bells are sure to chime.

Carol is in charge of a board and care facility where my father lived. She was really kind to my dad. When I was out with my dad one day, I pulled into a florist shop. He asked, "What are we doing here?" I told him we were getting Carol some flowers. He said, "Why?"

"Just as a gesture, Pop."

"She doesn't want any. She doesn't need any."

"How do you know, Pop?" When my Dad gave Carol the flowers and the card thanking her for all she had done for him, she was stunned. She said, "Things are tough around here, and it's not often someone goes out of the way to show his appreciation."

In the bouquet was a strand of tuberoses from Hawaii. That night Carol put the arrangement by her bed. During the night Carol kept getting scents of the tuberoses, reminding her of a trip to Hawaii. Right, Pop, she didn't want any flowers.

Nugget: Use flower therapy often, even if there is no occasion.

How: Pick up the phone and order them or pick them up at a store. If you're in doubt as to what to order, ask the florist. He or she will know what's fresh and appropriate from the available selection. This is their business. One flower can sometimes be enough. A hand-picked bouquet can create romance.

Chapter 48

Planning Romance

Many men confuse attention and romance. They aren't the same. Yes, attention is important, but showing attention doesn't always equal romance. Most women are hopeless (hopeful) romantics. This is woman's gift to man.

There are romantic and sensitive guys, but they are in the minority. If more men planned more romance, their lives would be easier. A lot of guys are not comfortable with women's ideas and images of romance. They think it's a conspiracy by the card and flower folks. The point these guys are missing is that truly romantic gestures show you have gone out of your way to say you care.

In their discomfort, people sometimes become sarcastic. Sarcasm comes in many forms. It can be lighthearted and humorous, or it can fit one of Webster's definitions: "to tear flesh." If you have been told in the slightest way that your sarcasm is not appreciated, **stop it!** You have gone beyond the point of being cute and funny. By continuing, you ruin any chance of serious romance in your life. Then it won't matter what you do to show romance because your partner will have withdrawn the really sweet feelings and emotions that romance is built on. They know by your track record that no matter how nice you try to be, you're going to destroy it with sarcasm. You have no idea how much of that others person's life you are missing by holding them under the threat of sarcasm.

If you are the one who has been living with sarcasm, do you really want it to stop? Then it's time to stop dropping hints or beating around the bush. Give concise, clear and direct signals about how you really feel (see Chapter 8). Don't hold back anything. If you can't tell your partner, write a detailed letter describing how you have been hurt by sarcasm. Let him/her know how he/she can win your heart back. You can demand an apology and the guarantee that it will never happen again—**never!** When the desired change takes place, be quick to reinforce it with praise.

Our good friend Karen is like many women who are still disappointed, waiting for their knight-in-shining-armor husband (or guy) to come riding in on a white horse, sweep them up and take them away to a romantic place. Karen's husband Barry, like most men, doesn't have a clue. Karen thinks, "If he really loved me he would know what I want!" How could he? Most people can't take you where they haven't been.

Karen feels that if she did more than drop hints (which Barry is not getting anyway) and told Barry what to do and how, the romance would be lost. Most of us men, however, need just this type of training-wheels advice. Give us the tasks, the time line, resources, and the learning curve with critique along the way. Reinforce the correct behavior so it will be repeated, and describe the potential **big rewards** that are waiting at the end of the rainbow.

According to a Lindt & Sprungil survey, 85% of people say they are romantic. Forty-two percent say they spend $10 or less per week on romance.

According to a Roper report poll of 1,994 adult women, here are the top five most romantic gestures:

A weekend getaway	55%
Long-stemmed roses	50%
Candlelight dinner at a restaurant	47%
Other flowers	32%
A love letter	31%

Other romantic things include a secluded picnic for two, sunrise and sunset, a moon-lit beach, and champagne or wine. What are romantic gestures for you?

I never used to give my wife Harriet love letters. I do now. I've learned how important they are for romance. Here is one I wrote when I was away on a speaking engagement:

Dear Harriet:

I'm at the fabulous Grant Hotel in San Diego. I'm in the restored dining room having a wonderful dinner, a glass of wine and enjoying the atmosphere. It just hit me that there is something missing. It is **you**. I realized how important it is to me that we share our lives together.

I miss you.

I love you,

Bobby

Well, I got a whole lot of mileage out of that letter. But that's not why I did it. I meant it. That's probably what made the difference.

Tom and Jill's life, like all of our lives, was hectic and stressed. They were finally going to get away and go on a vacation to San Diego. Tom had made all the arrangements. They had packed for the warm climate. When they arrived at the gate at the airport, however, Jill discovered that this plane wasn't going to San Diego. It was destined for Hawaii. That little devil Tom had planned a romantic getaway in Maui. Did it work? Aloooooooha!

Our anniversary is August 29th. In February of our thirtieth year, we were in San Francisco shopping. Harriet found a set of diamond and ruby earrings at Continental Gems Jewelers. She wanted them so badly, she said they could be her anniversary gift. I wouldn't have to get her anything else in August (which was probably not true).

Although the earrings weren't too expensive, they were more than I was prepared to spend. I called the jeweler Lily the next day and worked out a better price. Lily asked, "Shall I hold them?"

"Please," I said.

Three times that week Harriet begged me to call and get those earrings. I finally told her I had called and they were gone. It was true, I had them. I was showing them to her friends.

I gave them to her on Mother's Day. She was stunned.

On our anniversary we were going to Yosemite. The only accommodations available were tent cabins at Curry Village. I had been calling a couple of times a day for months ahead trying to get reservations at the Ahwahnee Hotel. Eventually, I got a room for Thursday and Saturday nights, but I couldn't get one for Friday. I called the concierge, whose name was Kathy. She checked the computer and said everything was booked. So I told her about our special occasion and how great it would be to celebrate it at the special anniversary/honeymoon table in their dining room. Kathy said, "You can't reserve tables in the dining room; they are on a first-come basis." When I called the Ahwahnee again the next day, the reservation person said, "Well, Mr. Smith, you already have a reservation for Friday." I asked him who made it? "The concierge." I immediately sent flowers to Kathy.

We arrived late on Thursday night. As I passed the turn for Curry Village, Harriet said "Where are we going?" As we turned into the Ahwahnee, she asked, "Do we have a reservation here?" I said, "Let's see".

Our reservations were in the romantic cottages behind the main hotel. There were flowers and a fruit basket with a card from Kathy. When we opened the drapes the next morning, we were amazed by the panoramic view.

I had told Harriet we would be having dinner in the Ahwahnee dining room on Friday night so she could bring something nice to wear. I requested that she bring those great anniversary earrings. She would have liked to have known we were staying at the Ahwahnee Hotel, because she would have brought different clothes. I won't make that mistake again.

When we arrived at the dining room on Friday night, there were three couples ahead of us. The chances of getting the anniversary table dimmed. When the couple ahead of us stepped up to the reservation desk, they asked if the best tables were given on a first-come basis. They were told that was true. "Well", I thought, "there goes our table." I watched as they went down the long hall. Then, at the last second they turned to a table on the left. We stepped up and said, "Reservation for Smith." The maître d' looked up and smiled. "Ah, the Smith's. Happy Anniversary." Kathy had told him. "We have a wonderful table for you." We were taken to the alcove at the end of the long hall to the anniversary table. Through the tall window we could see Yosemite Falls.

As we were enjoying these moments, a little black box appeared on the table. Harriet said, "What is this?" I looked puzzled. "Gee, I don't know." She opened it to find the ring that matched the diamond and ruby earrings she was wearing.

If you don't plan, you don't go.

Nugget: Romance, Romance, Romance is the life-blood of a relationship. Lives and kingdoms have been made and lost by love and romance.

How: Learn from each other what might be romantic for you. Use your imagination. Be creative. Build on what works for you. This takes planning. Be consistent. If you want ideas, get *1001 Ways To Be Romantic* by Gregory J. P. Godek. Phone toll free (800) Love-026.

Chapter 49

Cards and Spoken Gifts

Whenever Harriet had a birthday or if it was our anniversary or some other special occasion, I would get a humorous card for my wife. I couldn't relate to the serious cards.

For our anniversary a few years ago, I was trying to find an appropriate card. One of the cards I looked at was filled with all kinds of "forever I love you's, through the years, how much you mean to me, darling." I love you to the 10th power. It was so icky sweet that it stuck in my hand. I thought I would get it as a joke. When Harriet opened the card, I was kind of chuckling to myself. When Harriet looked up, she had tears coming down her cheeks. Did I get the message. You bet I did. This was no joke.

Now I don't wait for a special occasion. If I run across a nice card I get it. In fact, I keep several on hand for when I find the right time, or just any time I feel like expressing my love to my wife. I even send cards to friends and relatives or to someone who did a kind gesture or did some good work. I've been amazed by the responses this has elicited.

I've been known to give three or more cards to my wife on her birthday or on our anniversary. I leave them where Harriet will find them, or I send them in the mail, or I have a waitress bring a card out at a restaurant.

Some of my most cherished possessions are cards. One is from a mother thanking me for helping her son prepare for a police department oral board (he got the job), stepping in for his father who had died.

Another was from our friend Bill thanking us for showing that someone really cared about him in this world.

Still another was from John for his appreciation in sharing some thoughts on a struggle I had also faced.

The best card, though, was from our then 26 year-old-son, Rob, on my 50th birthday. It read, "Dad, from your #1 son. The help and guidance you have given me has put me in a place early in life where I feel I can say **I made it**. The feelings of contentment that I have for the past and future are largely due to you. Thank you. Love, Rob (your son)." I'm overwhelmed every time I read this card. All past sins are forgiven, son.

Phil, Elisa and Phil's Dad

Phil and Elisa fell in love. One week Phil came to San Francisco on business and Elisa came along also. I picked them up at the airport and we went to breakfast. While Phil was conducting business, Elisa and I explored Union Square. I said, "Let me do the dad thing and take you on a shopping spree." I was surprised when she hesitated. I assured her my offer was genuine. Elisa had trouble getting into the mode until I asked a salesperson to help. Then, hangers were being pulled off racks three at a time and taken into the dressing room. Elisa looked darling in some of the outfits, but I could tell she was still uncomfortable.

Elisa would be the first one to tell you she came from an unhealthy home. Later, Phil told me she had never been taken out shopping like that before. To make matters worse, her relationship with her dad had been horrible. So here I come in wanting to be the dad and take her on a shopping spree. No wonder my gift was hard for her to accept.

Phil and Elisa's romance blossomed. They got engaged and moved back to our town. They struggled financially, and Phil asked to borrow some money. We gave him only enough to carry them over, because we wanted to see them make it on their own.

A few months after they had their jobs, their situation improved. They wanted to take us out to dinner. During dinner, Elisa gave us a beautiful card. Inside was a check for some of the money they had borrowed and this note from Elisa, which I read aloud:

Dear Mom & Dad,

Thank you so much for all of your love and support. We would never have made it without you. You've filled so many needs in my own life and I don't know what I would do without you.

Mom, your concern for my health and happiness has really touched me. You have filled an empty spot in my life. It's kind of nice to receive a little "mommy concern."

Dad, words can not express my gratitude. You have filled a void that I never really thought could be filled. I never realized how important a daddy is to a girl. I've needed a daddy for a long time and you've filled so many of those needs. I don't know of any way to show my appreciation other than one thing. (Here is where I started to loose it.) Dad, I couldn't think of anyone else to give me away to your son at our wedding than you. (Every one of us was in tears then. And I am again as I'm typing this.) I'd be honored to have you by my side when I walk down the aisle. Will you give me away at our wedding?

I don't need an answer now. If you'd like to think about it, I'd understand.

I love you both so much. I don't know what else to say but thank you.

Love, Elisa

Thinking back, all we did was love Elisa like a daughter. Apparently, that is all she needed. Isn't that what we all need?

Spoken Gifts

Most of us don't do enough to let people know how we really feel about them. We've all been to a funeral and heard the testimonies of how great and wonderful the deceased person was. It's a shame. Wouldn't it have been great if that person really knew how people felt about him when he was among the living?

We miss great opportunities in complimenting people on how they impact our lives and the lives of those they touch. Often this is a way of showing God's love to those who might be resistant to His message. It validates to them what they have done and it encourages them to do more.

🔥   *A timely word is like apples of gold in a setting of silver.*

Oh, we have good intentions about planning to do this, but the time never seems to be right or we don't seem to think of just the right words. The time might never be right. Instead, we must take the risk of expressing our feelings before the window of opportunity is missed. People might move away or die and we would have forfeited a chance to express our love and appreciation.

In this process of expressing our gratitude to others, we, too, get a boost in life as the giver. It's a way of comforting one another.

This is how we did it in our family. My brother's 50th birthday was coming up. He had lived alone for fifteen years since his divorce. I called him to ask what his plans were for the Big Five-O. He said, "No plans yet, but don't worry about me. No big deal."

Since my brother never had children of his own, he had "adopted" the five nephews and three nieces of my three sisters and brother. He would take them on day trips, camping outings and mini-vacations, which these kids would never have enjoyed had he not taken the time. He even arranged for the entire family to be together at Yosemite.

My brother and I are eleven months apart in age. We're the products of "meet the rhythm brothers, Bob and Larry." We both had chicken pox on top of measles at ages four and five.

At my birthday celebration a month before his, Larry mentioned that he wished he had been able to purchase his high school yearbook. The seed was planted.

I arranged to have Larry's 50th birthday celebration at a local restaurant banquet room. The brothers, sisters, nephews, nieces and our dad were all there. Our mother had passed away five years earlier.

I alerted everyone that there would be an opportunity to tell Larry how he had influenced their lives. This could be a time for celebration and family healing. It sure was!

I started out by saying that in addition to being my brother Larry had also been my best friend when we were growing up. I then asked if there were any other comments.

There was a pause, then came sister Judy. "I'm not good at getting up and making speeches. I have to think things through and write them down." (A good way to handle this situation.) Judy proceeded to tell Larry what a special person he had been to her children: always checking in, arranging outings, sports events, circus outings, school meetings and other exciting plans and activities. Larry started to tear up.

Then it was like the many drops that produce a waterfall of love. Brother David said, "How great it is to have you as a brother." His wife Janet said, "The boys admire you and look forward to your calls and outings." (Larry once had camped out with the boys in their front yard.)

Then Mark my nephew stood up.

There is no telling where Mark would be now if it wasn't for Larry. When Mark was twelve, he had fallen so far behind in school he was cutting classes and heading in a dangerous direction. Larry made a commitment to spend time with Mark by tutoring him, setting out goals and incentives for him, offering rewards, and making him accountable. It took many hours, but it paid off. Mark had even received an award at his junior high school graduation for the most improved student of the year. Mark told Uncle Larry, "You'll never know how much you mean to me." These sentiments were echoed by sister Cathy, Mark's mom.

"No plans yet. Don't worry about me. No big deal, I'll find something to do on my birthday," Larry had said the month before.

Then Mark and Derrick got up and presented a rap musical routine to Larry which was appropriate from them.

Then something happened I didn't know anything about. All the nieces and nephews got up and went to the head of the table where Larry was sitting. They presented him with a plaque that read, "To the Greatest Uncle Who Has Done So Much For Us. Keep It Up. We Love You." I can't remember ever seeing my brother cry before. He did, then, however.

Then came the cards and presents. After my birthday I had placed an ad in the "Items Wanted" section of the city newspaper where we went to high school. "Wanted . . . Yearbooks . . . Tech High 1958 and 1959." (I wanted my yearbook, too.) Just as the ad was running out the call came in. We had the yearbook for 1958. Seek and ye shall find.

Larry guessed by the size what his present was before he tore off the wrapping. The relatives hooted and hollered as they located his pictures (and mine) in the yearbook.

I had asked Larry what kind of cake he wanted. "Oh, don't go to all that trouble." It was a great tall chocolate-with-whipped-cream-frosting beauty, with 50 half-inch candles. When the waitress brought in the cake, it lit up the room and you could feel the heat. Larry cried again.

At the end of the activities Larry said, "This is the best party I've ever had." We would have missed a great opportunity if we had not shared God's love with our brother. "No plans yet. Don't worry about me. No big deal."

We can really share life's joys by sending cards and giving spoken gifts to those around us.

> *Do things for others and you'll find your self-consciousness evaporating like morning dew on a Missouri cornfield in July.*
> **—Dale Carnegie (1888–1955)**

Nugget: Send cards and give spoken gifts to those family members, friends, workers and other people who touch and influence your life.

How: Do it now while it's fresh. Don't wait until tomorrow. Tomorrows have a way of never coming.

Chapter 50

Take the Mystery Out of Gifts

"Gifts" is one of the guesses that men make when they are asked if they know what makes women feel loved. Ironically, gifts does not rate high on the list when women are surveyed. Cards, notes and surprises are higher on the list. When asked, most women completing the survey reply that gifts are okay, depending on the intention of the giver. Some women, however, feel that gifts can be a form of control and manipulation.

A true gift is one without a hidden agenda. One that you don't have to reciprocate. The gift most important to most women is the gift of time and personal attention: "He listens to me." "He accepts and validates my feelings."

Gifts, however, were often on the list of the men surveyed. Not only are gifts on their lists, it is often written out exactly as "receiving or getting small gifts."

While on a trip to a secluded lodge in Lassen National Park, I gave the surveys to those people who were interested in helping with our research. I had become friends with Mike and Ayn during the previous two years we had been to Lassen Park. Ayn became ecstatic when Mike shared his survey list with her. After fourteen years of marriage, there on his list was something about which Ayn had no clue. The item was simply "getting small gifts."

Sometimes gift giving is the ultimate test to find out if that special person really knows you. Relationships are made or broken on the strength of the right gift, especially if you have been totally disappointed previously. Four out of five men can't remember what they got their partners for Christmas last year. The dead-wrong gift can be a turning point in a relationship; the right-on gift can be a rebirth of a faltering relationship. The right gift is one that you take the time, trouble, and careful research to find and reflects your understanding of your special person's interest.

Even when women drop hints to their guys, they still get disappointed when they don't get the gift they really wanted. A lot of guys feel the pressure is on to perform the magic. Ladies, forget the thought **if he really loved me he would know what I want.**

End the misery.

Take the poison early.

Just tell him.

You're the one responsible for getting the gifts that you want. I know it's not romantic, but you must go beyond the hints that aren't working and tell him you really want that big diamond ring.

If the gifts you want aren't arriving consider these options:

- ❤ Take your partner shopping and show him several possibilities. Then, be surprised which one you get.
- ❤ Make sure your partner knows your sizes and the colors you like.
- ❤ As my daughter-in-law Nancy leaves a store after seeing something she likes, she tells her husband Rob, "That was a medium."
- ❤ If you have your partner with you, be careful what you say. He is not your girlfriend. My wife would say, "That's cute." My guy radar would go on. I

would come back later and get it. Now, Harriet says, "That's cute. But don't get it for me."

💙 If someone doesn't come forward with the gift you want, as long as its not going to affect the national debt or put a burden on you to pay if off on plastic money, get it.

I was talking about the above in a coffee shop and Dorothy said, "My husband just gave me a birthday card that read, 'I found the perfect gift for you.' Inside it read, 'Let's sit down and I'll explain why we can't afford it.'" Cute, Eh? Dorothy went out and got what she wanted!

Don't go giftless. There was a hot restaurant in a town near us. On a lark we just drove over to see if we could get in. While we were waiting another couple came in without a reservation. The guy looked frazzled. They were celebrating their 18th wedding anniversary. We were both turned down. I asked where they were going next. They said a little French restaurant close by. We went over there to see if we could get in. We could, but the wait was an hour. It was already 8 p.m. In desperation, the other couple took the reservation. It was this guy's 18th anniversary and he hadn't bothered to make a dinner reservation!? His wife was standing there holding a gift and a card for him. He had nothing, not even a card. He was trying to laugh it off about not having a reservation, a gift, or a card. His wife was not amused. What do you think? Any meaningful romance after dinner that night? Ah, no.

I was talking to Frances after a Valentine's Day speaking engagement. She told me that she had wanted this ring for Valentine's Day. She went as far as cutting the ad out of the paper and sending her husband off to get it. He came back with a different ring. Same price. She asked him, "Why didn't you get me the ring I wanted?" He said, "I didn't like it." He wasn't going to wear it.

After talking to Frances, there was no doubt that her husband went back into the **penalty box**. And guys, you don't want to be in the penalty box, because you don't get **sex** . . . not even maintenance sex.

Stefani shared with a group I was speaking to that for her it doesn't always have to be an expensive or elaborate gift or flowers, just something that shows he cares. She told the group that her boyfriend had been out of work for some time and had just started another job. On Valentine's Day he took white shoe polish and wrote a special love note on her front window in reverse so she could read it. Stefani said, "That was worth more than any roses."

It was getting close to Christmas and Harriet asked me what I wanted. I just dropped some hints thinking she would figure it out. I wanted a computer to help me do this book. Under the tree appeared a big box, the size a computer comes in. On Christmas morning I started opening up the present with the anticipation of putting my manuscript on disc. Was I shocked, because in my computer box was a huge world atlas on a stand that lit up. As you can read, I did get a computer. But I still kick myself for not going beyond the hints.

Often, gifts are given to smooth things over and get out of trouble. A clue here, guys, from my friend Denise: "When men purchase a gift to get out of the dog house, don't choose a permanent gift for the house. It will be a constant reminder of bad times. Forgiven maybe, but likely not forgotten. Consider a temporary gift with an appreciated apology."

Denise told me that she had wanted some artwork for her home for years. She knew exactly what it was. At the worst possible time in their marriage, her husband Dave repeated something that almost ended their marriage previously. He tried to recover from this disaster by finally presenting Denise the artwork she had always wanted. Although their marriage survived, the present did not stay out long. It has been packed away for years, seldom to be seen. Denise said, "Years later I still can't bring myself to put it out because I start reliving that difficult time."

A note to guys: if you have your partner on a tight budget, don't overwhelm her with lavish gifts. This sends a mixed message.

> **Nugget:** Examine your motivation for giving a gift. Only give appropriate gifts, even when you're in trouble.

> **How:** If you really want a certain gift, tell someone you really want it. Ask a friend or salesperson what would be appropriate.

🔥   *There are four things guys have trouble saying. I'm lost. I can't fix it. I'm sorry. I love you.*

A Special Gift

There is an air show in Hayward California each year. At the last show there were two World War II Bombers, a B-17 and a B-24. They were on their way to a larger air show in Watsonville, California, scheduled a couple of days later.

Fred, in his seventies, was still a pilot. He was out every morning walking around the B-24, stopping, and staring off in the distance. He flew in B-24's during World War II over Europe. Not only did he fly in B-24's, this was the exact plane he flew in. Fred still belonged to his old unit and would attend reunions. They knew the numbers of this plane and that it was being restored.

Just before the planes were to depart for Watsonville, the old flight jockey's wife and son told him, "Dad, you're going with them. We have made arrangements for you to fly to Watsonville in the B-24." The son said, "It was the first time I saw my dad cry."

What an opportunity to relive the past. A real sentimental journey. The two war birds took off with Dad in his original seat. They made a fly-by, flew out over the San Francisco Golden Gate Bridge, and down to Watsonville. Think Fred will remember this? You bet. Make Memories.

Five Nuggets for Successful Relationships

Simple Tools to Uncomplicate Lives

- ❤ Recognize, understand, and accept that men and women are *dramatically*, *dramatically* different in incalculable ways. We are constantly judging each other by our own quite different standards. What may seem crystal clear to you probably is not to your partner.

- ❤ Find out what makes that person in your life feel special or loved. Open a Love Bank Account and start making deposits of those things that make that person feel loved. You will receive the interest and dividends from the account.

- ❤ Make the transition from criticism, defensiveness, contempt, and stonewalling to a ratio of five positive moments to each negative moment in your relationship. The Love Bank can be the accounting system for the five-to-one ratio. The one negative moment is just as important as the five positive ones. The short-term misery will clear the air and add newness to the relationship.

- ❤ Know what you want. Condense it to 15 seconds or less. Is this realistic for the person you are with? If not, go back to the beginning; present what you want to your mate. Have your partner repeat back what he/she heard. You might have to go back and forth a few times before it gets translated. Make adjustments where needed. Write the expectation down so there is no amnesia later.

💜 Plan evenings out and getaway trips. Then, follow through and do them. If you don't plan, you won't go. It's not optional. For your own mental health, it's mandatory. Schedule them and put them on a calendar. The anticipation before and the memories after are priceless. Go first class once in a while. If you don't, your heirs will. Adopt the philosophy, *if you are not already on a trip, you are planning the next one.*

The grass is greener on the other side of the fence.
It's just as hard to chew.
You've got to mow it, too.
It's just different grass.

The above is from the audio tape series, "Fire Up Your Communications Skills."

To obtain more information, contact Fire/Relationship Seminars.

Phone (888) 238-3959 toll free; Fax (925) 846-9650;
E-mail: captbob@verio.com
Web page: www.eatstress.com

Chapter 51

How Long Is This Going to Take? Are We There Yet?

Well, what have you done so far that has worked? How long did it take for you to get here? How many tools do you already have in your tool box for establishing and maintaining healthy relationships? How sincere are you in making the changes needed to acquire and use the new tools? You can't go through this process as if you are taking up guitar lessons and then you drop out during the normal adjustment period because you think it's just too tough to learn.

There is no magic wand. However, our personality is not set in cement. We *can* change. Aristotle wrote, "Well begun is half done."

At age forty-six, and three years into his second marriage with a new young son, my friend Carl was shaking his head about what seemed to be a repeat of parts of his first marriage. He felt as if he were lost at sea without a compass. After receiving some of the Nuggets of Life from the Love Bank, Carl set out to put the theory to the test. Carl was shocked that the most often-seen items from our surveys ("he listens to me" and "he validates my feelings") were on his wife's list.

Carl's wife Pat seemed curious as to what had motivated

him to pursue those things that made her feel loved. What was important, though, was that Carl finally knew and was responding with deposits. The situation was improving. What he had been doing was making only occasional deposits and then coasting for awhile. This is the yo-yo syndrome that sends mixed messages. It can cause insecurities to arise in another person because one minute the person feels loved and the next minute he or she doesn't.

Some people think they can do a little bit of work on their relationship and then coast for awhile. It's like putting out the spot fires as they occur. In my work as a firefighter, it's known that time and money are best used in fire prevention. If we concentrated on just fire fighting we would never catch up. It's the same in our relationships.

It could be compared to running down to the bank on a regular basis to cover bounced checks. It's the same thing with that special person's Love Bank Account. You can't limit yourself to making Love Bank deposits only when the account drops into insufficient funds. This situation creates the real roller coaster ride.

Some people have more commitment to a perfect payment record for a three-year car loan than they do to their special person's Love Bank Account. What Carl didn't realize was that Pat was constantly making withdrawals from the account and he needed to be faithful in making the regularly needed deposits to keep the Love Bank available for Pat's withdrawals. This is like having a certificate of deposit (C.D.) with a future maturity date. If you cash in the C.D. before it matures, there is a penalty for early withdrawal. The Love Bank has a similar penalty for early withdrawal.

But the dynamics would be far worse had you never opened a Love Bank Account. This is a lifestyle change. It is attacking the biggest single cause of divorce in this country, which is the inability to change personal selfish behavior. It is going from self-centeredness to other-centeredness. The dividends compound in the Love Bank Account at a higher rate, far beyond your imagination, and are unaffected by the world economy.

Believe me, there will be times when you will be reluctant to make the necessary deposits and use the new tools. It's like trying to hold out your cash deposit for a special purchase somewhere else. But you can't acquire the new tools and leave them in your tool box. They will rust. You need to use them on a regular basis to keep the skills up. It takes trust and a certain amount of risk. But once you get into the habit and have made the lifestyle change to follow through, it really works. It's like being let out of prison early for good behavior.

The Love Bank is not a destination that once you get there, you are done. (Silly you.) It is an ongoing journey.

You can do hard time or you can do easy time. The choice is yours.

> **Nugget:** Acquire and use the Nuggets of Life (skills) you need from this book and other resources. Use these skills to break down the barriers that will allow you to change your personal behavior. You can do it. You won't die.

> **How:** There were two frogs that fell into a bucket of cream. They started splashing and jumping around trying to get out, without success. As they became tired one frog said, "We're not going to make it." The other one said, "Just hang in there and we will make it." The tired frog finally gave up and drowned. The

surviving frog was committed and hung in there for the long haul. Suddenly the cream started to get thicker. It took less effort to maintain the frog's position. Then the cream turned to butter and the frog hopped out.

Such is life.

 Act as if it were impossible to fail.
—Dorothea Brande (1893–1948)

Chapter 52

Peace and Happiness

We have a small flower garden in front of our house. It's my piece of dirt. It's a color spot I enjoy. It didn't just happen. It took work, experience—and tools. First, I had to prepare the ground, then wait for the frost to end, select the variety of plants from what was available and, finally, use Vitamin B while transplanting to insure that the new plants would take hold.

If there were any existing blooms on the plants when I transplanted them, I had to snap them off because they would sap so much energy and nourishment they would threaten the chances of the plants making it through the shock period. Once the plants recovered and were producing new flowers I had to continue to remove them as they matured or else they would have gone to seed and the plants would have stopped producing new flowers. This process also strengthened and enlarged the plants.

There's a very similar experience in nourishing relationships. If we are not constantly cultivating, fertilizing and watering our relationships, they will become seedy, dry and withered.

At one point when I first started my garden the plants weren't producing many flowers. I checked everything. I had fertilized, watered and removed the mature flowers. All the necessary steps had been followed. I asked Harriet what was wrong. The answer: I needed to water more and cultivate the ground to allow the water to penetrate the soil to get to the roots. Within days after more watering it was like the horn of plenty. Color was everywhere. Again, like our relationships, we might have the necessary elements but in the wrong amounts for the harvest to take place.

Many people desire the nurturing relationship that produces a garden. They want their garden to attract the butterfly of peace and happiness. But just like trying to catch a beautiful butterfly that seems to dart and flutter away, it escapes their grasp right at the last minute because they probably don't have the necessary Nuggets of Life to catch it. It was that way for me. It was the Nuggets of Life that I acquired on this journey and my experience in using them and putting things in place from my past that produced an internal garden of peace and happiness.

With all the frustration, anxiety, depression and retooling that went on, I thought things would never really change. Then came a two-week period in July. I can't tell you exactly when it happened, but all the pieces of the puzzle came together. I wasn't chasing the butterfly of peace and happiness. I was just standing calmly and this beautiful butterfly of peace and happiness landed on my shoulder. There was no anxiety or depression, and they have seldom returned. I felt like the turkey when the red bulb pops out. I was done, and I knew it.

This is my prayer for you, friend.

 Hope is hearing the music of the future. . .
Faith is dancing to it today.

Appendix A

The following pages contain responses from men and women to the survey question, "What makes you feel special and loved?" These are suggestions you might be able to use in filling out your survey. The responses are in no particular order.

Men's Survey List

Acceptance	Meaningful conversation	Space (my own)
Attention	Support	Communication
Affirmation	Listening	Encouragement
Hugs	Touches	Trust
Compliments	Friends	Favors
Respect	Romance	Honesty
Acknowledgment	Recognition	Appreciation
Remembering	Cards and notes	Loved
Validation	Sharing feelings	Kisses
Sharing	Doing things together	Being held
Togetherness	Nurturing	Cheerful attitude
Caring	Sincerity	Kindness
Patience	Understanding	Happy home
Warmth	Gentleness	Being close
Back rubs	Having meals prepared	Family
Intimacy	Getting along	Thoughtfulness
Touching	Concern for one another	Being heard
Sensitivity	Affirmation	Time freely given
Being on time	Praying for me	Friendships
Humor	Unconditional love	E-mail

Commitment   Good looking   Peach cobbler
Reinforcement   Take time with me   Invitations
Forgiveness   Looking nice for me   Being needed
Unmerited praise   Praying with me   Surprises
Saying I Love You   A tone of voice   Compassion
A Look   Returned phone calls   Faith
Tenderness   Being cared for, doted on Loyalty
Truthfulness   Assurance   Security
Faithfulness   Shared goals   A love fax
Something done without asking
Home environment

Women's Survey List

Attentiveness	Affection	Communication
Patience	Thoughtfulness	Sharing
Cards	Hugs when I'm stressed	Presents
Sensitivity	A love fax	Togetherness
Appreciation	Compliments	Thank you's
Always included	Acceptance	Validation
Respected	Flowers	Notes
Encouragement	Invitations to dinner	Concern
Touching	Someone cares about me	Affirmation
Nurturing	Phone calls or notes	Giving
Words that say so	Care when I'm hurting	A real hug
An invitation	E-mail	Listened to
Giving	Helping around the house	Responding
Trust	Affection without sex	Tenderness
Cheery hello	Saying I Love You	Little things
Understanding	Being treated special	Humor
Fellowship	Setting the burglar alarm	Loyalty
Gifts of love	Generosity	Eye contact
Prays with me	Pride	Promises kept
Being a giver	Getting things fixed	Romance
Gentleness	Romantic adventures	Courteousness
Freedom	Focused attention (listening)	Caress
Back rubs	Support in my decisions	Not being judged
Just talking	Financial security	Protectiveness

Open communication

Accepting my faults

Knowing he'll do anything for me

Willingness to help with chores

Being thought about during day

Praise in presence of others

Interest in what I'm all about

Hear my name in conversation

Helps without being asked

Appendix B

There Is a Lot More to Learn About Money
(Continuation of Wampum)

The following is a smorgasbord of ideas for planning and saving your wampum. The further you read toward the end of this section the more sophisticated the plan will become. As deep as it might get, hang in there as long as you can. This will be a real education for many of you.

Only 27% of those surveyed in the College for Financial Planning said they could last more than six months if they or their spouses lost their jobs. One in five in the survey said they would be in deep financial trouble immediately if either they or their spouse were suddenly unemployed. Where do you fit in? Are you and your partner living hand-to-mouth? If so, close your "trap" and read on. Help is at hand.

Credit Cards

The religious part of Christmas really comes about 30 days after December 25, when you open your credit card bill. Then you say, "Oh, my God!"

It's almost a necessity to have a credit card in this Western society. Credit cards are used for identification. You can't rent a car without one. And they provide a convenient way not to have to carry money. Americans carry over 500 million credit cards. Many people have three to four bank cards, as well as gasoline, clothing store, and mail order charge cards.

More than a few people have felt the sting of this plastic money. To see something and buy it with plastic can create a monster.

The average balance for the under 30 group jumped 149% to $2,200 within five years. During the same period, the balance for adults rose 86% to $2,353. Some of this increase can be attributed to people charging more to get frequent flyer mileage and other bonus programs.

Credit card debt grew 26% over the last ten years. It could take a lifetime to pay off a $10,000 credit card bill by making minimum payments. The average interest rate is 19.8%

In a weak economy, people try to bridge the gap with credit cards, to maintain their status with the good life. Or when they get caught in downsizing they use credit cards to make purchases of equipment and cover payroll to start a business. CitiCorp earns $3.6 **billion** on credit card interest and collects $500 million in annual fees . No wonder credit card companies are always wanting to mail you their cards. For most banks, credit cards are the highest money makers. Some banks earn in the 50% profit range on their card operations.

If you had a $1,000 balance on a credit card that was charging 19% interest, how long do you think it would take you to pay it off making the minimum payment? About ten years. It would take longer as some cards drop to 3% on the amount that is applied to the principal.

If you have a large portion of your consumer debt in 20+% credit cards, you could be tied up and digging a big hole. And you can't deduct credit card interest on your taxes anymore. Being able to pay off your credit cards and not pay those high interest rates would be an instant savings plan. If you must have a card, try to pick one with a low or no annual fee and one that has a grace period on your purchases before interest is added on; usually 20 days to 25 days is allowed if you don't have a balance from the previous month. Shop for a credit card as you would any major purchase. Then select the credit card that represents how you use credit.

Thirty-six percent of credit card holders pay their card balance off every 30 days. The rates are high to those who don't pay off their balance. They carry the cost of operations for those who pay off their cards early.

If you can't pay off your card in a timely fashion, make more than the minimum payment. This won't change the interest rate, but every dollar you pay over the minimum balance is one fewer dollar for which you will be charged on your next billing.

If you are having trouble making your credit card payments, call the company and ask for their reduced interest rate plan for an extended period of time. Also, ask that your due date be changed to the middle of the month so you don't have all your bills due on the first. They would rather have a payment with a reduction in the interest rate than no payment.

Many people are switching credit cards to take advantage of the introductory teaser of a lower interest rate. When the card is scheduled to raise to the standard rate in six months, they jump to a new card with yet another teaser rate. These people are finding they eventually get rejected for any credit request because their credit reports show a prostitution between mutiple open lines of credit. Unless you have a plan to retire the debt, don't start switching ponies.

Want a gold card? This is a perfect example of status. It's like you can own part of the Gold Mine. What really happens is the bank gets the Gold Mine and you get the shaft. The Golden Rule: Those who have the gold make the rules.

How's Your Credit?

There is a one-in-five chance that there are errors on your credit report that are damaging enough to keep you from qualifying for a loan. There is a 50-50 chance that there is an error of some kind on your report. Consumers Union conducted a survey of 161 reports from TRW, Equifax, and TransUnion, who produce most of the nation's credit reports. Errors ranged from mixing relatives' data, not showing all creditors, balances that had been paid off, and releasing data to unauthorized parties.

Applying for credit is not the time to find out there are problems with your credit report. Trying to unwind this web can cause delays in your current financial plans, frustration and embarrassment. You should check your credit every year or so to make sure all is well. TRW information systems (800) 682-7654 provides one free credit report per year. A report from other companies costs from $3 to $20 depending on what state you reside in. If an error is on your report, notify the credit agency. They are required to contact the creditor and remove the wrong information if it is not valid. But this can take up to six months. Be persistent. Your good credit is the cornerstone and your ticket to the best interest rates and terms. A poor credit report will send you to higher interest rates. Bad credit can follow you for a long time. Those who defaulted on their student loans are now hostages to the consequences.

When I worked for a consumer financial firm, it seemed once a person got off to a good start with banks, S&Ls and credit unions, he or she stayed on that path with good credit. Those who started off with storefront finance companies and thrift institutions, stayed on that path with poorer credit, even though they had the income to get better financing. With good discipline your credit can be improved and maintained.

Need Money?

The best time to line up money is when you don't need it. That's right. At your leisure you can do the credit applications and the other support information and have pre-approved credit at your disposal. Many lending institutions and credit unions have this service available. Many have unsecured personal lines of credit that you can establish to cover short-term needs. Please don't wait to try to set up credit when your wife is pregnant and your income is on the downside. Do it on your terms.

Who's your banker? If you don't know, you should. Having an established relationship with the person at your bank who has the gavel to approve your needs is mandatory. You don't want to be facing a stranger someday when you really, really need a loan. I marvel at people who stick with their same large, stodgy, no-service bank that has turned them down for loans. The banks that seem to provide the best overall service are the smaller regional banks.

Buying a New Car?

Most people going in to buy a new car think they can pull one over on the salesman. These guys are experts. They do it all day long. You don't stand a chance unless you follow some basic rules. This is usually the second most expensive purchase you make after your home. Although most salesmen (I'm being kind) are fair, there are some that would cheat their mother or eat their young. You can work the dealer like he'd like to work you.

Why can't the price be the price? Well, some cars are being sold at one price. These vehicles are sold at about an 11% markup. You can usually buy a car for about a 6% markup.

Before buying a new car consider buying the same car from one of the rental car agencies. They could have the same year vehicle with ten to twenty thousand miles on it and $5,000 less than the new one at the dealer, along with a warranty and a copy of the service record. The new car dealers hate the rental car sales so much, they have forced the car manufacturers to buy back a high percentage of the rental cars and distribute them throughout their used car lots. I suggested to a friend that she look at the rental car sales before buying a new one. She said she liked the smell of a new car. I promptly went down to the auto supply store and bought her an aerosol can of "New Car Smell." She saved $5,800.

If you are going to try to buy a car from a rental car company the price can be negotiated. They try to lead you to believe the price is the price. It isn't!

If you really need to buy a new car, insist on seeing the dealer invoice. If they won't show it to you, leave. I asked to see one at a dealer recently and was told that it was against their policy to show the invoice. I said, "I guess we have nothing to talk about," and left. By the time I got to the curb, the salesman came flying out with the invoice. It's kind of like, who gets whom by the nose first. Once they find out that you know what they know, the games will end. Dealing directly with the fleet manager will often prevent the games. You can find out in advance what the dealer's invoice price is by picking up a copy of Edmund's *New Car Guide*.

Once you have the invoice, ask what discounts are being offered by the manufacturer in addition to any factory rebates. Most manufacturers are now allotting the dealers an amount on each vehicle. It is up to the dealer to decide how to best use the money in discounts, advertising, or financing to sell the cars.

Get the flat, naked price. Don't try to plug in tax and license, since they will always be constant. Once you know that price, start using the following guidelines to negotiate.

Negotiating Tips

There are few worse feelings than having your first offer accepted.

Whenever you are attempting to make a purchase where the price is not fixed on a car, home, boat or whatever, consider using these tips to pay a fair price.

1. He who cares the least wins.
2. The first person to mention a figure loses. Let the other person mention a price. Their price might be lower than you were thinking.
3. When the other person mentions a price, pause for a while.
4. Then offer a much lower price. Just the price. Then shut up, no matter how much you want to say something.
5. If they say, "I can't do that," pause, and then say, "What can you do?"
6. Once they mention that price, pause and say, "I'll meet you halfway."
7. Repeat Step 5.

Be prepared to walk away. Don't get lot fever. Don't get the hook buried. Whose money is it? Right, yours! Don't forget.

If the salesman is a friend or has been recommended, people tend to drop their guard when buying a car. Be cautious. Follow the procedure no matter who the salesperson is.

The last car we bought for our college son we knew the price ahead of time (Edmund's *New Car Price Guide*) and saw the dealer's invoice. The factory was allocating $800 to the dealer. We settled on $400 below invoice! That gave the dealer $400 to split with the salesman on a $15,000 car, and we got the warranty at their cost. That's right, their cost. Most people don't know that the warranty can be a negotiated item. With all the electronics on the new cars, the warranty is a good investment. Try to negotiate the warranty to their cost. If you sell the car you can also sell the warranty to the new owner or cancel the warranty and get a refund.

For used cars, buyer beware. Check the "Blue Book" and have the car looked at by an experienced service agency. If you have the opportunity to attend an auto auction, you might find a deal. But be careful not to get caught up in the frenzy.

Personal Experience by Julie

I was in the market for a new car. A customer who comes into my shop to get her hair done recommended a car salesman at the dealership where she works. I went down figuring I was going to get a good deal with the referral. On the way home, after filling out the contract, I got a sick feeling in the pit of my stomach that something was wrong. That was a lot of money just for a new-car smell.

The next day I had a friend call the salesman asking to see the invoice price. The salesman said the contract was pretty close to the invoice price. My friend said, "Well then, you won't mind us coming down and looking at the invoice?" The salesman's reply was, "Er, uh, well, what have you to do with the purchase of this car?"

My friend said, "Well, if I tell her not to buy the car, she won't." The salesman understood that statement real quick.

I was scared as we arrived at the dealership. But once we saw the invoice statement I was shocked. After some quick negotiating my friend got a new sales price that was $2,400 less than the previous deal I had made. I was so disturbed about how I was deceived I ended up not buying the car.

Your Tax Man

Don't expect your tax preparer or accountant to give *you* any sage advice on your financial planning when you go into do your taxes. To start with, there is nothing that can be done to help you for the year that just passed—the one you're filing taxes for. That year is in cement. And your tax guy is going to be so frazzled by the time you show up late to do your taxes (the average accountant's cholesterol rises 100 points during tax time) that he's not going to be much help to you. And if he had such a great plan, he wouldn't be telling you, he would be doing it himself.

So, once the shock has worn off after you write the check to the IRS, you kind of ease back into your lifestyle until next tax time.

Do a personal tax work-up every September to estimate where you're going to be at year end. If any mid-course corrections need to be made, you have plenty of time.

Analysis Paralysis

I've seen people analyze an investment with such intensity they end up becoming paralyzed, turning to stone, and not making a decision. They become afraid of the risk. Life is a risk every day. Even the right decision is wrong if it's made too late. You'll never be able to know 100% of what you need to know on any venture. But somewhere between 50% and 75% should put you in enough of a comfort level to act one way or another so you won't miss the window of opportunity.

We have a friend, Larry, who continually over-analyzes every investment move he makes. He ended up losing in an apartment house partnership in Oregon and when he finally exhausted himself investigating diamonds that were being touted by a so-called friend, he bought in and the market promptly went into the tank. The guarantee to purchase the diamonds back at the original price disappeared.

I work with a friend Steve. A year and a half ago Steve finally bought his own home and fixed it up. Now his property is worth $70,000 more than he paid. Steve could establish a line of credit for investments using the property as security. But Steve is afraid to risk the opportunity. This is $70,000 he didn't even have two years ago and now he is scared of losing it. Yes, I know, each of us has his or her own comfort level. But couldn't we invest just a teensy bit, please?

   The secret of success in life is for a man to be ready for his opportunity when it comes.
   —Benjamin Disraeli (1804–1881)

Deferred Compensation Plans (401Ks)

Deferred compensation plans (401Ks) are one of the best investments going because they use pre-tax money from your paycheck. These are tax-free employer plans. You will pay the taxes on this money when you take it out of the plan or retire. Of the 40 million employees eligible for 401K plans, only 23 million take advantage of the programs. The average balance is $32,000.

If you are in a 28% federal tax bracket, pay 9% state tax, and earn 10% on your 401K plan, that's 47% you have saved in taxes and earned in interest and dividends. If you invest heavily enough in a 401K plan and change your payroll tax deductions, you won't lose any money. This is like finding money in the street. My son Rob is putting $300 a month in a 401K plan. Because of how it has adjusted his taxes, it works out to be only a $150 contribution on his part.

This is where reinvesting the money you were sending in taxes to Washington, D.C. comes back to you and really pays off. The limit you can invest is around $8,475 a year. The limit is adjusted each year to match the cost of living. If your employer does not have a plan, encourage him to start one. The minimum cost is a great employee benefit and it provides golden handcuffs for employees.

Plans vary. They can have one to ten categories in which you can place your money: stocks, bonds, mutual funds, second deeds on real estate, annuities, money market accounts, investing in your company stock and more.

Where you place your money will depend on your comfort level, your risk tolerance, your age, and motivation. Most people don't take enough risk in these plans, especially younger employees who can recover from any short term setbacks. Investing in the company you work for probably is not a good idea. You probably wouldn't want to sell the company stock if times got bad for your company.

The beauty of these plans is **dollar cost averaging**. In both good and bad markets you just plod along and continue to invest in the program. This is the most proven method of getting the best return. When the market is down your money will buy more shares. When the market goes up, you are already in position with the shares you bought at the lower prices, not waiting for the market to take off before jumping in. It will cost more to buy new shares when the market is up, but overall dollar cost averaging can work in your favor. Combine dollar cost averaging with compound interest and you will have lots of horsepower.

If you get into a 401K plan, there will come a time when the return on your investments (that's the ROI) will be more than what you put in. If you contributed $1,000 a year in your 401K plan and earned 10% interest, you would have $200,000 after 30 years. That is $86,000 more than a taxable investment if you were in the average tax bracket.

Employers can match a portion of your contribution. Like most savings plans, the best time to initiate or increase your investment is when you get a raise or promotion. If you haven't been getting it until now, you probably won't miss it if you don't see it.

If you just take the new money from a raise or promotion as additional salary, then try to save it, you will soon find out that you don't have any of that new money left to invest unless you are careful.

You'll just be transferring more around. You might have more funds to put in your 401K plan than you realized. Many companies now offer their employees cafeteria benefit packages. The employees are given a set amount that they can use according to their needs, from medical to 401K plans. My friend Mike was using his $350 a month from his cafeteria benefit package for his medical plan when his wife had a suitable medical plan with her employer that they could use. They switched to her medical plan and the $350 a month ($4,200 a year) that Mike was using for his medical plan is now going into Mike's 401K plan.

There are four ways to get your money out of a 401K plan. Leave the company, retire, suffer a hardship, or die. I don't recommend the last.

Are You Living in Your Own Home?

Even if owning your own home is not being considered the investment that it was in the past, it is one of the last bastions to write off on your taxes.

Although there are comparisons favoring renting to buying, the thrust there is to be able to take the savings by renting at a low amount and wisely investing the difference. How many people, however, would be successful in really getting the money invested? Statistics reveal that Americans are saving only 4.5% of their after-tax income .

In addition to still being a forced piggy bank, a home fulfills a domestic need for the family (see Chapter 28).

You might have more resources for obtaining a home than you think. There are banks, S&Ls, VA, FHA and "For Sale by Owners" who want to sell you a home with as little as 5% down. Lenders provide classes to help first-time buyers through the maze. The listings are out there, you just need to do the legwork to locate them. If you set your goal to own a home you will get a real education in the process. There are still assumable loans around that you don't have to qualify for. It might not be the home of your dreams in the best area, but you won't be staying there forever anyway.

Many areas have bond financing for first-time home buyers. Qualifications vary from area to area.

You might be depriving a relative of the opportunity and enjoyment of giving you the down payment for your own house. Get a plan together, know the amount you need, swallow your pride and just present your desires. I've seen this work countless times.

Rental Property

If you own your home, do you have what it takes to own rental property? Many don't. If you can't say "no," or can't ask for the rent when it's late, stay away from becoming a landlord. If you **can** do these things, this can be a great way to build your financial base. Here are two examples of taking $20,000 and putting it in savings or a rental home.

20,000 Savings	120,000 Home
6%	6%
$1,200	$7,200

If you put the $20K in savings, it will pay $1,200 the first year. You will have to pay taxes on the interest. If you put that same $20K into a $120,000 home at 6% appreciation, the increase is $7,200, not considering the depreciation and other write-offs. The government is basically paying you in lower taxes, to buy rental property and maintain it.

That's just the first year; run this equation out five years! At five years, with a 6% increase a year, the home would be valued at $160,585. You would have recovered your $20,000 investment within two-and-a-half years. You would have paid taxes each year from the interest on your savings. You didn't pay taxes on the amount you increased the value of your rental home. As the value of your rental property increased, you could refinance the property and take money out without paying taxes. (You could buy another rental property with the money.) The only time you will pay taxes on the rental property is when you sell. If you trade the property, the taxes are deferred. Meanwhile, the rent on the rental property is increased each year. This is leveraging. You can't do this with any other investing. This is only one house. What if you had five homes? Would you be paying taxes? Probably little, to none. Is it legal? Absolutely!

The real secret to renting is to get the right tenant into your property. Careful screening of the tenants' applications will keep the bad guys out. Don't short-cut this process, no matter how fast you want to get the place rented.

Renting to friends, relatives or your kids could be a big mistake. You have to operate your rental property like a business. How could you handle late rent payments or even an eviction of a relative, friend or your own child? Many people say, "Well, what if the place goes empty for two months?" I say, "How many people died on your block of malnutrition last year?" Good rental property at a fair market rent doesn't go vacant. The sky is not falling, Chicken Little.

The ideal rental home is a 3-2-2—three bedrooms, two baths, two car garage. I can rent these cookie cutter homes every day.

I'm not guaranteeing that managing rental property will be easy, but it is one of the best ways I know of to make money.

> 🔥 *Flaming enthusiasm, backed up by horse sense and persistence, is the quality that most frequently makes for success.*
>
> **—Dale Carnegie (1888–1955)**

Vacation Rental Property

Many people consider vacation rental property as their first income property. They justify the investment by being able to use the property themselves. How perfect. I would suggest that unless there is a strong domestic need . . . rent, don't buy. Buy your rental property close to you and rent in the area you are considering for vacation property. The return on your investment will be higher.

We owned a vacation rental property. During any one year we went up to our chalet for only twenty-two days. Even after the tax advantages that was still $232 per day it cost us to use our own mountain retreat. You could go to a lot of places for $232 a day. This is not even considering trying to keep it rented during the off-season and maintaining it from 125 miles away. Management companies didn't do any better. Some play favorites, leaving your property empty.

There was also the feeling that if we had the place in the mountains we were kind of locked in to going there for vacation or whenever we got a chance to get away. This prevented us from traveling to some other great places.

We sold our vacation property to friends who also rent it out. We can still rent our retreat at a lower price than when we owned it.

Time Share Ownership Property

Harriet's 86-year-old Aunt Lois Dawson said she won't live long enough to get dumb enough to purchase a time share. She's right! Although it might work for a few of the 1.8 million time share owners worldwide, unless there is an unbelievably strong domestic need to own a time share, stay away.

To start with, there are absolutely none of the tax write-off advantages of real estate.

Just a quick look at the numbers will tell you why there is all the hoopla and magic type showmanship at these sales presentations. If you figure that the average ownership of one week is selling for $8,000, and you multiply that times 52 weeks, you get a total of $416,000 per unit. (They tell you they only sell fifty weeks and use the other two weeks of the year for maintenance. I don't think so.) Multiply $416,000 by the number of units in the time share project and we're talking megabucks and huge commissions.

They will tell you that you can trade your time share week for another time share unit anywhere in the universe. But it seldom turns out that way. You see, unless you have your week in the prime time for your area (they usually distinguish the time periods by colors) no one is going to trade his or her good week with you. Even if you have the desired period, the trades don't always blend.

The profits for these operations can be so large they offer attractive packages to lure you in to take the bait.

My friend Chuck came up to me one day and said he hoped he hadn't done the wrong thing. He had bought a time share at Lake Tahoe at a hyped-up presentation in San Francisco, and he hadn't even seen it. He let them take it back on default after less than two years. He is one of the armies of people who want to get out of this obligation but then find out there is virtually no resale market. There is such an urgency to get out, there is currently a scam that tries to get unsuspecting owners to pay $250 just to list with the scam.

They also tell you that you can stay in a unit at your complex and around the world wherever there is space available at a per-day reduced rate because you are an owner. What they don't tell you is you can get the same deal if you aren't an owner. So, why buy?

One of our firefighters, John, got an invitation in the mail for a time share presentation in Lake Tahoe. Just for showing up he would receive a gift. John was going up to Tahoe with his cousin George and their wives anyway, so while they were up there he wanted to go by and get his gift. John's wife didn't want to go to the presentation, so he took George. The gift turned out to be a camera, but you had to have your wife with you for the presentation to collect the gift. John just told them George was his wife. They asked them where they were from. San Francisco, was the reply. They gave them the camera!

Equity Lines of Credit

If you own your home you could be sitting on an untapped gold mine. The equity in your home could provide you with tax deductible resources.

Eighty percent of the value of your home, less what you owe in mortgages, is usually a guide for what lenders will give you on a home equity line. If your home is worth $120,000 and you owe $60,000 in mortgages you could receive an equity line of $36,000. Always try to get the maximum that you are qualified for on an equity line, as it usually doesn't cost any more.

Equity lines work like a credit card. Once you set one up

you only pay interest on the amount you have out. You can pay them off anytime. This is far more flexible than having a straight second mortgage with fixed payments from day one.

You can use the money from an equity line for anything you want. You can invest it, buy rental property, pay college tuition, travel, buy consumer goods, fix up your home or car, pay off your credit cards, put in a pool—whatever you want.

Although you can no longer write off the interest on auto and other consumer loans, you can write off the interest if these items were purchased with the equity line from your home.

The limit you can write off for an equity line on your taxes is $100,000 more than the original purchase price of your home, plus any medical or education costs.

There are some people I wouldn't tell about equity lines. Before you know it they would have a new Ferrari or be in Hawaii.

Shop around if you want an equity line. With the competition you can usually find lenders offering packages with little or no fees.

C.D.'s vs. Money Market Accounts

I've seen many people park their funds in a one two or three-year certificate of deposit trying to get a higher rate. At the same time, I've seen safe money market accounts with about the same rate and the flexibility of no pre-payment penalty and a checkbook and/or credit card to gain instant access to their money. If you don't need your money for the required extended period of time of a C.D., you're okay. But you might be able to have both worlds: a good interest rate and flexibility in a money market account.

Stocks and Bonds

You're on your own for this one. If you have the interest, skill, and the tolerance, go for it. Some people do really well at chasing the rabbit down the different trails.

Consider a good mutual fund for stocks or bonds that has a good track record over the years. Don't just pick the one with the best record last year.

Limited Partnerships

Are you among those who learned how limited partnerships worked in the 1970s and 1980s? They started out with the General Partner having all the experience and the Partners having all the money. When they ended up the General Partner had all the money and the Partners (you) had all the experience.

Often, these are easy to get into and almost impossible to get out of.

If you are still trapped in a partnership, there is now a market where you might be able to get out. You might have to take a haircut, but at least you could take the loss and have your money to reinvest. Expect to lose up to 35% of your investment.

First, try to sell to your General Partner. You might get your best offer there. If that fails, call Liquidity Fund at (800) 833-3360. It buys limited partnership units for itself or for pension investors.

Business Partnership

If you are considering going into business with someone else, you better think long and hard about it. Partnerships are the most common form of business. Also the most fatal per capita. Especially with a relative. According to my C.P.A. Mike's experience, most marriages last longer than most partnerships.

Everything's great in the honeymoon period just like in a World War II era movie. All these people with lots of energy suddenly get up and put on a big review show.

The honeymoon soon ends. There are long hours, more money needed than was anticipated, finger-pointing at who's not doing as much of the work, and the other members of each other's families getting involved. Save yourself the hassle. If you've got a good plan, do it yourself. And don't think just because you have a great skill that you are also going to be a good businessman. You probably don't know all of what it takes to run a business. It will probably take a longer time than anticipated to turn a profit. And even then, you aren't laughing all the way to the bank. You can't be an absentee owner. You become married to your business.

If someone else wants in, let him or her invest money only, at a good return, with no expectation of ever getting it back if the business doesn't make it.

Most businesses fail because they are under-capitalized (not enough money going in until the business starts earning a profit). Many people fail because they get into a business they know nothing about. Only one in ten businesses makes it past the first year. Only three in a hundred earn more than an average income. And you're working long hours.

You should really know your motivation before you invest. Realize the time and money that will be needed before going into business. If you are considering buying a business, remember this: If you don't have a good solution to the potential problems that exist in that business (oh yes, there are problems in every business) these problems will become **your problems.**

If you absolutely have to go into business with a partner or are buying a property with partners, write down (have an attorney do this) every detail you can think of going in. Who's putting up what, working when, job descriptions, and how to buy out and/or when you are going to sell. Believe me, this could turn ugly and be worse than any divorce.

References and Suggested Reading

Austin, Dr. Glen M. 1988. *Love and Power: Parent and Child.* California: Robert Erdmann.

Berman, Dr. Henry, Louisa Rose, and Lynne H. Williams. 1987. *The Too Precious Child.* Nashville: Atheneum.

Berry, Carmen Renee. 1988. *When Helping You Is Hurting Me: Escaping the Messiah Trap.* San Francisco: Harper Collins.

Brock, Barbara, "Intuition Is a Part of Business," *Daily Review,* (30 June 1990).

Canter, Lee, and Marlene Canter. 1982. *Assertive Discipline for Parents.* New York: Harper Collins.

Carpenter, Liz. 1994. *Unplanned Parenthood: The Confessions of a Seventy-Something Surrogate Mother.* New York: Random House.

Castleman, Michael, "De-stress Your Love Life," *Prevention,* (June, 1991).

Godek, Gregory J. P. 1995. *1001 Ways to Be Romantic.* Weymouth, Massachusetts: Casablanca Press.

Gottman, John Ph.D.. 1995. *Why Marriages Succeed or Fail.* New York: Fireside/Simon & Schuster.

Gravitz, Herbert L., and Julie D. Bowden. 1985. *Recovery.* New York: Simon & Schuster.

Hensley, Dr. Dennis E. 1991. *Moneywise.* Eugene, Oregon: Harvest House

Klavens-Simring, Sue, and Steven Simring. 1991. *The Compatibility Quotient.* New York: Fawcett Press.

Mayer, Anne. 1990. *How To Stay Lovers While Raising Children.* Price Stern Sloan.

Menrith, Dr. Frank B., and Dr. Paul D. Meir. 1978. *Happiness Is a Choice*. Michigan: Baker House.

Mackay, Harvey. 1988 *Swim with Sharks Without Being Eaten Alive*. New York: Morrow.

Miller, Keith. 1991. *A Taste of New Wine*. New York: Arbor House Spring.

Patterson, James, and Peter Kim. 1991. *The Day America Told the Truth*. New York: Harper Collins.

Peters, Thomas. 1982. *In Search of Excellence*. New York: Harper Collins.

Pond, Jonathan. 1991. *Safe Money in Tough Times*. New York: Dell Books.

Index

If you have thoughts, comments or ideas about *Fire Up Your Communications Skills*, I would enjoy hearing from you. You can write to me at:

"Captain Bob"
5565 Black Avenue
Pleasanton, CA 94566

You can send an E-mail to: captbob@verio.com

My web site is www.eatstress.com

Order Form
Fire Up Your Communication Skills

☐ Yes, I would like to order _____ books at $14.95 ea.
+ shipping + applicable sales tax.

I understand that I may return any books for a full refund,
for any reason, no questions asked.

☐ Unedited audio album from live speaking engagements $12.95.
☐ Combo pack of audio album and book $23.95.
☐ I would like information on quantity orders.
☐ I would like information on a speaking engagement.
☐ I would like information on one-on-one coaching
(in person or via phone).

Fax orders:	(925) 846-9650
Telephone orders:	Call toll free (888) 238-3959
On-line orders:	captbob@verio.com
Mail orders:	Code 3 Publishing, Captain Bob, 5565 Black Avenue Pleasanton, CA 94566, USA Tel: (888) 238-3959 toll free

Name: _____

Address: _____

City: _____ State: _____ Zip: _____

Telephone: (_____) _____

Sales Tax:

Please add 7.75% for books shipped to California addresses.

Shipping:

$4.00 for the first book and $2.00 for each additional book.

Payment:

☐ Check
☐ Credit card: ☐ VISA,   ☐ MasterCard

Card number: _____

Name on card: _____ Exp. date: ___/___

Call toll free and order now
(888) 238-3959
Web Site: www.eatstress.com

Order Form
Fire Up Your Communication Skills

☐ Yes, I would like to order _____ books at $14.95 ea.
+ shipping + applicable sales tax.

I understand that I may return any books for a full refund,
for any reason, no questions asked.

☐ Unedited audio album from live speaking engagements $12.95.
☐ Combo pack of audio album and book $23.95.
☐ I would like information on quantity orders.
☐ I would like information on a speaking engagement.
☐ I would like information on one-on-one coaching
(in person or via phone).

Fax orders:	(925) 846-9650
Telephone orders:	Call toll free (888) 238-3959
On-line orders:	captbob@verio.com
Mail orders:	Code 3 Publishing, Captain Bob, 5565 Black Avenue Pleasanton, CA 94566, USA Tel: (888) 238-3959 toll free

Name: _____

Address: _____

City: _____ State: _____ Zip: _____

Telephone: (_____) _____

Sales Tax:
Please add 7.75% for books shipped to California addresses.

Shipping:
$4.00 for the first book and $2.00 for each additional book.

Payment:
☐ Check
☐ Credit card: ☐ VISA, ☐ MasterCard

Card number: _____

Name on card: _____ Exp. date: ___/___

Call toll free and order now
(888) 238-3959
Web Site: www.eatstress.com